Psychoanalytic Sex Therapy

Psychoanalytic Sex Therapy: Exploring the Unconscious Life of Sexuality bridges the gap between depth psychology and modern sex therapy, offering a fresh, integrative approach to understanding sexual struggles.

Rather than treating symptoms like low desire, intimacy challenges, or compulsive behaviors as dysfunctions to fix, this book reveals how they often carry emotional meaning linked to trauma, attachment, and unspoken conflict. Drawing on compelling clinical stories and contemporary theory, Juliane Maxwald helps clinicians decode the unconscious narratives behind sexual concerns. Chapters explore topics such as desire discrepancy, pornography, consensual non-monogamy, erectile unpredictability, and narcissism, demonstrating how the thoughtful integration of technique and depth-oriented insight can foster real change. Grounded, accessible, and clinically rich, this book invites therapists to listen to sexuality not just as behavior, but as a window into emotional life – and as a story the psyche tells through the body.

This is essential reading for psychotherapists, psychoanalysts, and sex therapists seeking to deepen their work with issues related to sex, intimacy, and relational life.

Juliane Maxwald, MA, LP, CST, is a psychoanalyst and certified sex therapist in New York specializing in sexuality, trauma, and relational dynamics. She teaches and supervises nationally across psychoanalytic and sex therapy settings.

Psychoanalytic Sex Therapy

Exploring the Unconscious
Life of Sexuality

Juliane Maxwald

Routledge
Taylor & Francis Group

NEW YORK AND LONDON

Designed cover image: Getty Image © natrot

First published 2026
by Routledge
605 Third Avenue, New York, NY 10158

and by Routledge
4 Park Square, Milton Park, Abingdon, Oxon, OX14 4RN

Routledge is an imprint of the Taylor & Francis Group, an informa business

© 2026 Juliane Maxwald

ISBN: 978-1-032-33098-3 (hbk)
ISBN: 978-1-032-32730-3 (pbk)
ISBN: 978-1-003-31818-7 (ebk)

DOI: 10.4324/9781003318187

Typeset in Sabon
by Apex CoVantage, LLC

"Sexuality, Desire, the Unconscious, the Unspoken! Finally, the connections are being made. This is a groundbreaking book that has been a long time coming. It warmed my heart and stimulated my mind."

Mark Epstein MD, author of *Going to Pieces without Falling Apart and The Zen of Therapy: Uncovering a Hidden Kindness in Life*

"This book is a sterling addition to the growing movement within sex therapy toward integrative relational practice. Maxwald demonstrates a deep appreciation of both conscious and unconscious sources of desire, arousal and erotic connection. Her cases come alive as she deftly describes common challenges that lead, under her wise guidance, to pathways of transformation. Clearly written, she makes psychodynamic sex therapy not only accessible but compelling. A must read for psychoanalysts who want to better understand sexuality and sex therapists who want to understand the psychodynamics of sexuality."

Suzanne Iasenza, PhD, Author, *Transforming Sexual Narratives: A Relational Approach to Sex Therapy.*

"Masters and Johnson may have taken the field of sex therapy from Freud to the laboratory, but Juliane Maxwald, with her modern psychoanalytic perspective, puts sex therapy back on the couch and shows us that everything old is new again. Her book Psychoanalytic Sex Therapy: Exploring the Unconscious Life of Sexuality is a meaningful contribution to the literature and sure to deepen the toolset of any clinician working with sexuality"

Ian Kerner, sex therapist and NY Times best-selling author of She Comes First.

"Juliane Maxwald takes you deep into the mind of the psychoanalytically oriented sex therapist. Wonderfully written with a heavy reliance on case studies, Maxwald has made a substantial contribution to the next wave of sex therapy. This is a book that I will most certainly be recommending to both my sex therapy trainees and seasoned colleagues."

Daniel N. Watter, Ph.D., Past-President, The Society of Sex Therapy and Research (SSTAR), author *The Existential Importance of the Penis: A Guide to Understanding Male Sexuality.*

"Psychoanalytic Sex Therapy: Exploring the Unconscious Life of Sexuality is a deeply honest and provocative dive into the undercurrents of sexuality. Juliane Maxwald leads readers into conversations that few have had but all of us need, particularly through a psychoanalytic framework. It is a first of its kind read on the shadow side of sexuality within a solidly clinical lens. Bravo Juliane!"

Holly Richmond, PhD, author of *Reclaiming Pleasure: A Sex Positive Guide for Moving Past Sexual Trauma & Living a Passionate Life*

"In her elegant and incisive debut, Psychoanalytic Sex Therapy: Exploring the Unconscious Life of Sexuality, maverick therapist and psychoanalyst Juliane Maxwald does what many thought impossible: she explores sexuality and desire through a psychoanalytic lens while dispelling the tired notion that such work must be sex-negative, pathologizing, or dull. This brave book marks a bold new era for those of us integrating psychological wisdom and sexual intelligence into our healing practices. With a voice that blends clinical expertise, scholarship, compassion, and unapologetic power, Maxwald offers a much-needed—and deeply welcome—contribution to the field."

David M. Ortman, author of *Sexual Outsiders: Understanding BDSM Sexualities and Communities*

"Juliane Maxwald's new book, *Psychoanalytic Sex Therapy,* dives into a much-needed discussion about sexuality, intimacy, and meaning. Clinicians and members of the broader public will benefit tremendously from this warm and wise invitation to aliveness and connection."

Alexandra H. Solomon, PhD, licensed clinical psychologist, faculty at Northwestern University, bestselling author of *Love Every Day,* and host of the podcast, *Reimagining Love*

Contents

Preface

The stories in this book are drawn from my work as a psychoanalyst, couples therapist, and sex therapist over the past two decades. While the clinical material is based on real therapeutic encounters, every effort has been made to protect the privacy and dignity of my clients. Names, identifying details, and timelines have been altered, and in many cases, stories are composites – woven together from themes and experiences that have emerged repeatedly in my practice.

These are not formal case studies. They are narrative reflections, grounded in the emotional truths that reveal themselves in the consulting room: the shame that hides beneath desire, the longing beneath anger, and the fear that often sits behind avoidance. Though the particulars of each story are unique, the struggles they depict are strikingly common – and profoundly human.

My intention is not only to illuminate the therapeutic process but also to make space for a deeper public conversation about sexuality, intimacy, and emotional life. I hope these stories serve as a window into the complex, tender, and often transformative work that takes place when we speak the unspeakable and listen beneath the surface.

Introduction

My Journey – From the Couch to the Consulting Room: How Psychoanalysis and Sex Therapy Came Together

Foundations: Discovering Psychoanalysis

Sex: Three little letters that form such a powerful word. The word carries enormous weight in our personal lives and in our culture at large, connoting everything from pleasure to shame, connection to isolation, vulnerability to power, our most intimate moments to the brash commercialism of "sex sells." For many years, my professional life has centered around understanding the complexities that these three letters represent.

Psychoanalysis has always been my first love. I discovered it during my time in art school, where I began exploring the unconscious – those most unknown and enigmatic parts of our minds. Psychoanalysis seduced me with its promise of accessing deeper layers within myself and others. What might lie beneath the surface? In art school, I explored themes of sexuality, the body, and identity, and was drawn to questions about the depths of the self – all themes that would continue to fascinate me throughout the next 25 years of my life. This book represents not an end point, but rather a pause in my ongoing journey – a moment to reflect on the relationship between my sex therapy training and my psychoanalytic background, sharing the insights I've gathered along the way.

This book is for clinicians who want to deepen their understanding of sexuality through a psychoanalytic lens, and for anyone curious about how talking about sex can be a doorway into healing and growth. Through clinical case composites, theory, and reflection, we'll explore how our sexual lives can illuminate the deepest layers of who we are – our histories, longings, conflicts, and potential for transformation.

Art school was my time of discovery – a way to find myself, express myself, and push boundaries alongside my fellow students who were on similar paths. It was indulgent, exciting, and liberating, yet also painful and lonely. I delved into the darker parts of my personality, uncertain of the outcome or whether I would survive (metaphorically speaking). I embraced the self-importance of this journey that only being a twenty-something

DOI: 10.4324/9781003318187-1

artist could allow. Most importantly, art school led me to psychoanalysis, as I found myself increasingly curious about why my fellow students and I created the art we did. What were we trying to communicate? Where did the impetus for creativity come from? What emotional wounds were we trying to probe, reveal, and overcome through the creative process?

These questions led me to The Center for Modern Psychoanalytic Studies (CMPS), where I experienced my own analysis while studying the theory and technique of the psychoanalytic process. Here I discovered that the beauty of psychoanalysis lies in its curiosity. The treatment room becomes a cocoon of exploration, with the couch providing insulation and safety, freeing the mind to roam wherever it pleases. Here, we discover parts of ourselves long-buried or forgotten. The tension between knowing and not knowing, thinking and feeling, frustration and gratification all rise to the surface and hover over the psychoanalytic process. The process of free association creates a landscape of thoughts, feelings, memories, and fantasies. This exploration can spark wonder and excitement or anxiety and horror, and sometimes both simultaneously.

Our defenses inevitably surface to protect us: our mind shuts down, we become distracted, preoccupied, our anxieties rise. This is the fundamental tension of knowing and not knowing – healing and truth trying to emerge while old defenses hold on, protecting us in ways no longer needed. The treatment room becomes a container for all these messy parts, making space for not knowing, for uncertainty, for the depths of our unconscious minds.

Sex and sexuality often become the landscape where this messy process plays out. Our unconscious manifests through sexual symptoms, anxieties, fetishes, fantasies, conflicts, and discrepancies. These symptoms are symbolic messages held by the body, trying to be understood. As Bessel van der Kolk reminds us, the body keeps the score. Often, these messages speak to attachment wounds and trauma, whether catastrophic experiences like abuse and neglect or the quieter bruises of developmental and relational trauma.

Psychoanalytic therapy perpetually asks, "Why?" It encourages us to explore the reasons behind our thoughts, reactions, and behaviors, often pointing us back to our family of origin for clues. What parallels can we draw from our past that appear in our present lives? Whose voice do we hear when we make assumptions about the motivations of our boss, our partners, our children, or the world at large? When we become curious about ourselves, we begin to widen and deepen the context of our lives, which provides us with a richer sense of meaning. The greatest gift from my psychoanalytic training was learning to listen with curiosity and delay action. Therapy becomes a space to be heard, seen, understood, and validated. When we feel listened to and understood, we feel safe. With safety comes trust, and with trust comes the freedom to explore who we truly are, who we might want to be, or rediscover the parts of ourselves that were exiled into hiding long ago. In trust lies eroticism.

From Psychoanalysis to Sex Therapy

As my practice evolved, I found myself drawn to couples therapy, where this therapeutic foundation took on new dimensions. Working with couples presented new challenges. Being a good listener wasn't enough – couples therapy required a more active approach. I needed to manage the negativity, aggression, pain, longing, and vulnerability of each partner so they could engage in the sessions and leave feeling contained. While psychoanalysis allows for delayed action, couples therapy often demands immediate intervention. Where psychoanalysis permits the therapist to dream and fantasize, couples therapy often requires constant alertness to hold, contain, challenge, and comfort each partner.

The therapist's body becomes more activated in couples work than in individual therapy, and it was this work that led me to sex therapy. Attachment needs form the undercurrent of couples work, with sex often becoming the landscape where these needs play out. Sex and sexuality serve as a portal to access memories, fantasies, longings, and fears. They can be an escape or a hiding place, containing the potential to both annihilate and celebrate as we embody our vulnerability and surrender to desires – our own or another's. Anxiety and shame often become bedfellows to sex, hijacking our ability to be present. Sexual symptoms frequently manifest as unconscious projections of anxiety and shame onto a partner, while sexual behaviors often represent unconscious attempts to overcome or master these feelings. Sex therapy helps people unpack and explore their sexual histories within developmental, biological, familial, social, and cultural contexts.

Historically, psychoanalysis has had an uneasy relationship with sex therapy. Early Freudian theory placed sexuality at the center of psychic life, yet the clinical practice of psychoanalysis has often distanced itself from the embodied, practical work that sex therapy entails. My own evolution as a clinician required me to bridge this gap – to bring the richness of psychoanalytic theory into the immediacy of working with sexual problems and to allow the body its rightful place in the therapeutic encounter.

This book emerges from my journey through the portal of sex and sexuality, reflecting the evolution of my therapeutic style. In recent years, I've explored the distinctions between therapy and coaching, fascinated by what enables people to change. Is it insight? Discipline? Self-reflection and mastery? Risk-taking? How does a therapeutic relationship promote healing and growth? Can mentorship and collaboration heal? Does it matter whether it's with a therapist coach or mentor? What role might spirituality play in healing, growth, and expansion? While these questions extend beyond this book's scope, their spirit of curiosity about healing, growth, change, and the interplay of thoughts, emotions, and behavior runs throughout these pages, simmering beneath discussions of relational dynamics and the social nervous system.

We live in a society that privileges the mind and rational thinking, revering productivity and accomplishment. We strive for control because it gives a sense of power and helps manage our anxiety – anxiety that often resides in us because we have unconsciously abandoned ourselves, bringing with it great shame. Power, control, and success help us feel connected to something meaningful, yet they never truly satisfy, becoming instead an addictive cycle of anxiety, shame, and control. The unconscious mind, with its inherent irrationality, doesn't concern itself with productivity or achievement. Our Id, where unfiltered wants and desires live, fuels our sexual energy and vibrancy. It's where we come alive and surrender, where we can lose ourselves in the moment and time stands still – if we feel safe enough to do so.

The Integration: Psychoanalytic Sex Therapy in Practice

My clinical work integrates psychoanalytic principles with individual therapy, coaching, couples therapy, and sex therapy interventions. Decades of interdisciplinary training and direct client experience inform my approach, drawing from various models: psychoanalysis and psychodynamic therapy, cognitive behavioral therapy (CBT), trauma work, addiction treatment, emotionally focused therapy (EFT), motivational interviewing, harm reduction, self-help groups, group therapy, the Gottman method, Imago, relational, interpersonal and intergenerational approaches, coaching practices and principles, internal family systems (IFS) and parts work, psychedelic-assisted psychotherapy, spiritual and energy practices, among many others. While learning has been a source of pleasure and motivation, the mind can only take you so far into sex and sexuality before the body takes over, refusing to be controlled or contained. As such, I began to notice the moments when language fell short and sensation spoke louder: a client dissociating mid-session, another flushed with excitement, another suffering under the grip of shame. These moments highlighted for me the limits of purely verbal insight and led me to integrate somatic and trauma-informed approaches. Psychoanalytic sex therapy is the culmination of all these clinical paths and represents the therapeutic dance between mind and body – like sex itself, it is the place where the two meet.

This book is rooted in a contemporary psychoanalytic framework that holds sexuality as deeply interwoven with unconscious life, relational experience, and the emotional body. Drawing on theorists such as Jessica Benjamin, Adrienne Harris, Stephen Mitchell, and Jack Morin, I explore desire not as a fixed trait or identity but as a dynamic expression of inner conflict, attachment history, and the longing for recognition. Rather than offering prescriptive models, these pages reflect a commitment to relational attunement, emotional complexity, and a tolerance for ambiguity. The overarching theme is what Bion might call the capacity to "sit in the unknown." Throughout the chapters, readers will encounter the analytic concepts of mutual recognition, core erotic themes, erotic differentiation, and the non-unitary self alongside research and ideas from contemporary sex therapy, including the work of Suzanne Iasenza, Lori Brotto, Ian Kerner, and Justine Lehmiller. Somatic and trauma-informed approaches – especially those of Stephen Porges, Peter Levine, Janina Fisher, and Bessel van der Kolk – also inform the clinical thinking, highlighting how desire is not only psychological but embodied. These theoretical threads are not presented as dogma, but as living ideas that weave through the case narratives, offering a multifaceted understanding of sexuality that is curious, compassionate, and grounded in clinical practice.

This book presents case studies illustrating common sexual issues that couples and individuals face today: desire discrepancy, low libido, painful sex, erection, ejaculation and orgasm problems, pornography and sex addiction, infidelity, kink, BDSM, consensual non-monogamy, and open relationships. You'll read about people struggling with confusion, shame, and frustration about their sexual selves, and the various ways we try to control our sexuality based on societal, familial, or religious judgments. You'll learn about trauma's damaging impact on sexuality, family-of-origin conflicts, and complicated relationship dynamics. Through these stories, you'll read about both the challenges and triumphs of individuals and couples as they navigate their sexual journeys.

Most importantly, you'll discover the transformative power of talking about sex. Each case study reveals how breaking the silence around sexuality can lead to healing, growth, and deeper intimate connections. As you read these stories, you may find echoes of your own experiences or gain new perspectives on sexual wellness and relationships. My hope is that this book not only illuminates the complexities of modern sexuality but also opens up space for more open and layered conversations about this fundamental aspect of human experience.

Chapter 1

From Silence to Discourse
Addressing Sexuality in the Counseling Room

What Brings Clients to Sex Therapy

Sexual concerns arise in therapy more often than is typically acknowledged, often hiding beneath more socially acceptable complaints such as relationship stress, anxiety, depression, or general dissatisfaction. Yet sexuality is central to many people's sense of identity, worth, and connection. When sexual difficulties arise, they are rarely confined to the bedroom; they touch on our most vulnerable psychological and relational patterns.

Historically, the field of sex therapy gained momentum through the pioneering work of William Masters and Virginia Johnson (1970), whose research and treatment protocols focused on physiological sexual response and behavioral modification. Their approach laid a foundation for subsequent generations of therapists, including Helen Singer Kaplan (1974), who integrated psychodynamic theory with behavioral interventions, introducing the now widely used model of desire, arousal, and orgasm as a framework for understanding dysfunction.

Today, clients may seek sex therapy for a wide range of concerns: discrepancies in desire between partners, challenges with arousal, orgasm difficulties, genital pain (such as vaginismus or vulvodynia), premature ejaculation, erectile dysfunction, compulsive or out-of-control sexual behavior, shame about masturbation or porn use, and the emotional aftermath of infidelity. Many also arrive seeking support with sexual identity development, gender transition, consensual non-monogamy, kink/BDSM interests, or healing from sexual trauma.

Importantly, some clients do not enter therapy identifying a "sexual issue" at all. Rather, sexual themes may emerge gradually through the therapeutic process. Clients often test whether the therapist is comfortable enough to receive sexual material. They may allude to a "lack of spark" in their relationship or express vague discomfort during physical intimacy. These are moments that require the therapist's attunement. When met with openness and curiosity, such disclosures can lead to transformational

DOI: 10.4324/9781003318187-2

work. When minimized or deflected, they may reinforce shame or deepen the client's reluctance to engage.

Moreover, many people come to therapy with long-held sexual scripts shaped by culture, family, religion, and media – scripts they may have never questioned. As Michael Bader (2002) noted in *Arousal: The Secret Logic of Sexual Fantasies*, our sexual preferences often reflect deeper unconscious conflicts and longings. In this view, sex therapy is not merely about "fixing" dysfunction but decoding the symbolic meanings of arousal, inhibition, and fantasy.

What brings clients to sex therapy, then, is not only what's not working – but a deep desire to understand themselves more fully. As sex therapy evolves, it becomes increasingly interdisciplinary, calling on therapists to address not just behaviors or symptoms, but the emotional, relational, and societal meanings of sexuality itself.

A Multi-Theoretical Approach to Sexuality in Therapy

Sex therapy has long drawn on behavioral foundations, particularly in its early development. Masters and Johnson's (1970) pioneering work laid the groundwork for behavioral treatment of sexual dysfunctions, emphasizing structured interventions like sensate focus to reduce performance anxiety and increase bodily awareness. Helen Singer Kaplan (1974) built on this work with her "New Sex Therapy," which integrated psychodynamic thinking with behavioral techniques. Her triphasic model – desire, arousal, and orgasm – reflected a crucial shift from purely physical to more psychological and relational considerations. These approaches remain essential, particularly for clients experiencing clearly defined physiological or functional concerns.

Yet sexuality is not reducible to function. Behavioral interventions can fall short when clients face issues rooted in deeper emotional, relational, or existential struggles. Contemporary sex therapy therefore demands a more integrative, multi-theoretical framework – one that holds space for unconscious meaning, attachment needs, trauma history, somatic experience, and relational dynamics.

Attachment theory, as developed by Bowlby (1969/1982) and extended into adult romantic relationships by researchers such as Hazan and Shaver (1987), offers a compelling lens through which to understand sexual behavior. Securely attached individuals tend to view sexual intimacy as a natural extension of emotional closeness, while those with anxious or avoidant patterns may find sex either hypercharged with need or fraught with discomfort. For example, a client with anxious-preoccupied attachment may seek frequent sex as reassurance of love, while their avoidant partner may retreat from sexual intimacy to preserve a sense of autonomy – creating a cycle that fuels conflict and misunderstanding.

Relational psychoanalysis deepens this view by emphasizing the intersubjective field between client and therapist. Stephen Mitchell (2002), a key figure in relational theory, viewed sexuality as inherently relational and dynamic – shaped by unconscious fantasies, cultural scripts, and the relational matrix in which one develops. Within this frame, a sexual symptom may serve as an encoded message about longing, fear, or conflict, not just a dysfunction to be "fixed."

In addition to attachment and relational theories, feminist and queer theory have been essential in challenging heteronormative and patriarchal assumptions embedded in traditional sex therapy. Authors like Judith Butler (1990), Gayle Rubin (1984), and Carol Queen (1997) argue that sexuality is performative, socially constructed, and power-laden. Their work urges therapists to question how norms about gender, desire, and "healthy sex" shape both clinical practice and client self-perception.

Finally, many contemporary clinicians are integrating somatic approaches, such as Hakomi, Sensorimotor Psychotherapy, and Internal Family Systems (IFS), which allow for access to preverbal and embodied memory. These methods recognize that many clients carry sexual trauma or shame not in words, but in muscle tension, breath constriction, or avoidance of touch. Somatic work allows clients to gradually reinhabit their bodies, cultivate safety, and differentiate between past threat and present experience.

Taken together, a multi-theoretical approach allows therapists to move fluidly between symptom relief, emotional exploration, and meaning-making. Rather than reducing sexuality to behavior or identity alone, it becomes possible to hold the erotic as a multidimensional, evolving expression of the self – one shaped by physiology, psychology, relationships, and culture.

Sexuality Across the Lifespan

Sexual development is not confined to adolescence or early adulthood – it is a lifelong process that evolves in expression, meaning, and capacity. One's erotic life may deepen, shift, or reawaken with time, and the therapeutic approach must be flexible enough to support these transitions.

Adolescents and Young Adults

In adolescence, sexuality often emerges amidst ambivalence, secrecy, and social pressure. Teens may face the challenges of identity formation, body image insecurity, consent navigation, and the early shaping of relational scripts. Many carry the burden of limited or misleading sex education – what Peggy Kleinplatz calls the "sexual mis-education" of youth – which can create distorted understandings of pleasure, safety, and consent. Early experiences may be influenced by trauma, exploitation, or coercion, which go unnamed or mischaracterized due to developmental immaturity and silence in families or schools.

In therapy, young clients may struggle to articulate their experiences in sexual terms or fear judgment for their questions or behavior. Clinicians must model openness, non-reactivity, and thoughtful curiosity. It is also critical to engage the broader systems shaping adolescent sexuality – peers, family, digital culture – while helping youth claim ownership over their emerging sexual selves.

Young adults, navigating autonomy, hookup culture, and online dating, often experience tension between emotional intimacy and physical intimacy. The pressure to perform, experiment, or "catch up" can generate anxiety or shame. Therapy can offer a rare space to explore desire free from external performance expectations, and to begin cultivating sexual self-awareness grounded in agency and authenticity.

Midlife Clients

Midlife is often a juncture of sexual recalibration. Hormonal shifts (e.g., perimenopause, andropause), career transitions, parenting fatigue, and long-term relationship dynamics all impact desire and sexual functioning. Some clients experience a fading libido or sexual discomfort for the first time, while others report a resurgence in erotic vitality after years of suppression. The psychosocial tasks of midlife – reevaluation, identity renegotiation, confrontation with mortality – can spark deeper inquiries about meaning, pleasure, and self-acceptance.

For partnered individuals, midlife is often when desire discrepancies come into sharper focus. One partner may feel disinterested in sex, while the other feels rejected or deprived. Clinicians can support couples in differentiating sexual behavior from emotional closeness, making room for new expressions of connection. Here, the therapist may draw on Esther Perel's work, which underscores the erotic paradox of safety and separateness: the idea that desire thrives not just in intimacy, but in mystery and individuality.

Older Adults

Aging does not mean the end of sexuality. While physical changes (e.g., slower arousal, vaginal dryness, erectile variability) are real, so too are new freedoms – freedom from reproductive concerns, from performance scripts, and sometimes from long-standing relational roles. However, the dominant cultural narrative of aging is desexualizing. Older adults, especially women and LGBTQ+ elders, often feel erased from sexual discourse.

In therapy, older clients may need space to grieve losses – of partners, of function, of youth – and also to reclaim erotic potential. Sexuality in later life may include more sensuality, more creativity, more experimentation, or a return to self-touch as a source of comfort and vitality. Therapists must remain curious, not prescriptive, about what sex means to each client across time.

The Impact of Culture, Religion, and Technology

Sexuality is never expressed in a vacuum. It is shaped, constrained, and expressed through cultural, religious, racial, technological, and systemic frameworks. A psychotherapist's attunement to these dynamics is not ancillary to sex therapy; it is essential.

Cultural Scripts and Sexual Identity

Cultural messages about sex begin early and often operate unconsciously. Clients may come into therapy carrying sexual scripts that were never explicitly named but deeply internalized: that sex is dirty, dangerous, sacred, or an obligation. These narratives influence not only behavior but also fantasy, arousal, inhibition, and shame. Drawing on Simon and Gagnon's (2003) theory of sexual scripting, therapists can help clients deconstruct the inherited roles and expectations shaping their intimate lives.

For clients of color, sexuality is often filtered through intersecting lenses of race, gender, and class. Black women may struggle with hypersexualized stereotypes like the "Jezebel" trope, while Asian men may confront emasculating messages of desexualization. Latina/o/x clients may carry cultural expectations around machismo or marianismo, which can create conflicting feelings about dominance, submission, and sexual agency. Therapy must make room for the ways racialized bodies are read, eroticized, and disciplined by cultural discourse.

Clinicians must also be mindful of their own cultural location and how it shapes the clinical frame. A white, cisgender, heterosexual therapist may unknowingly reinforce dominant assumptions about "healthy" sex or monogamy. Inviting dialogue about cultural meaning, rather than pathologizing difference, is a key stance of culturally competent sex therapy.

Religion and Sexual Shame

Religious frameworks can be both supportive and limiting. For some, spiritual traditions provide structure, community, and meaning, even within a sexually conservative ethic. For others, religion has been a source of repression, judgment, or trauma. Clients who grew up in purity culture, for example, may carry deep shame around masturbation, premarital sex, or same-sex attraction. Others may experience an internal split between their spiritual identity and their sexual desires.

Sex-positive therapy does not mean dismissing religious belief. Rather, it invites integration. Therapists can help clients explore questions like: What values do you want to carry forward? Which teachings no longer serve you? Can you reclaim a sense of sexual wholeness that includes, rather than excludes, your spirituality?

Clinicians like Kristin Neff and David Schnarch have emphasized the importance of self-compassion and differentiation in navigating these tensions – developing the capacity to stay grounded in one's values while tolerating difference within relationships, families, and cultures.

Technology, Porn, and the Digital Body

Technology has revolutionized how we connect, express, and eroticize ourselves. From dating apps to sexting to virtual reality, sexuality is increasingly mediated by screens. These platforms can offer new freedom – particularly for queer, disabled, or geographically isolated individuals – but they also come with new anxieties.

Online dating, for example, can amplify rejection sensitivity and promote a kind of "disposable intimacy," where people become profiles to swipe on rather than whole individuals to relate to. Clients may struggle with ghosting, compulsive matching, or the constant pursuit of novelty. These patterns can mirror unresolved attachment wounds, particularly in those with histories of abandonment or inconsistent caregiving.

Pornography, too, is often misunderstood in therapy. While some therapists still pathologize porn use, a more nuanced approach asks: *What role is porn playing in your erotic life?* Is it a tool for fantasy and self-regulation? A way to access desires that feel forbidden in partnered sex? A barrier to intimacy? As Michael Vigorito and Doug Braun-Harvey suggest in *Treating Out of Control Sexual Behavior*, the goal is not abstinence, but alignment – helping clients develop a sexual ethic congruent with their values and relational goals.

Clinicians should also consider how social media impacts body image, self-worth, and arousal. The pressure to be "sexy" or perform desire for others can erode internal erotic attunement. For many clients, especially younger ones, therapy becomes a place to relearn how to listen to their own arousal, rather than curate it for an audience.

Therapist Comfort and the Invitation to Speak

Despite increasing cultural openness about sex, many clients still carry the belief that sexuality is not appropriate to discuss in therapy. This belief may stem from prior therapeutic experiences, internalized shame, or fear of being judged. Clients often wait weeks, months, or even years before revealing sexual concerns – sometimes until the therapeutic relationship feels safe enough, and sometimes never at all.

This is why therapist comfort with sexuality is so significant. The therapist's demeanor, language, and even subtle body cues communicate whether sex is a welcomed topic. A client who notices a therapist visibly flinch, glance away, or rush past a sexual disclosure may internalize the message that their sexuality is too much, too taboo, or not relevant to their healing.

Therapist training in sexuality varies dramatically across programs. Many graduate programs offer little to no education on sexual development, sexual health, or the treatment of sexual concerns. As a result, therapists often enter practice with minimal preparation to address even basic sexual issues, let alone complex dynamics like kink, desire discrepancy, sexual trauma, or erotic transference. Without further training, supervision, and self-reflection, clinicians may unconsciously avoid the very material their clients most need to explore.

As Suzanne Iasenza (2020a) writes, "What makes someone a sex therapist is not their comfort talking about sex – it's their ability to be emotionally present when clients do." This includes knowing how to respond to silence, how to stay steady when clients describe fantasies or behaviors that challenge our values, and how to use our own internal reactions as a source of therapeutic insight.

Therapists must also examine their own sexual histories, identities, and biases – not to disclose them to clients, but to prevent them from unconsciously shaping the clinical encounter. This process may involve asking:

• What messages did I receive about sex growing up?
• Where do I feel confident in my knowledge, and where do I feel uncertain or uneasy?
• What kinds of sexual behavior do I find challenging, confusing, or activating – and why?

These reflections often bring us into contact with our own shame, desire, or blind spots. Supervision or consultation with colleagues trained in sex therapy can provide a space to process these reactions with curiosity rather than judgment. In doing so, we expand our capacity to hold space for the full spectrum of human sexuality.

Countertransference and the Erotic in the Room

Sexuality inevitably stirs the therapist's own subjectivity. Erotic material can provoke countertransference – conscious or unconscious emotional reactions based on the therapist's personal history, desires, defenses, or wounds. For example, a client's submissive fantasy may evoke discomfort in a therapist with a history of powerlessness. A couple's conflict around porn use may trigger unresolved tension in the therapist's own relationship.

These responses are not problems to be eliminated, rather they are opportunities to be explored. When explored mindfully, countertransference can become a diagnostic tool. As Patrick Casement (1991) suggests, the therapist's internal experience often contains clues about the client's unconscious communication. Erotic countertransference in particular requires thoughtful containment, supervision, and interpretation.

Some reactions may signal overidentification: a therapist who unconsciously aligns with a client's sexual shame or takes a partner's side in a sexual dispute. Others may indicate avoidance: a therapist who "talks around" erotic material or reflexively redirects the conversation. By bringing these dynamics into supervision or peer consultation, therapists can differentiate between what belongs to the client and what belongs to themselves.

Working with sexuality in therapy also invites the therapist to inhabit their own body. This includes becoming aware of physiological responses, for example, tightness, warmth, numbness, or arousal – and understanding how the therapist's body is participating in the relational field. Somatic countertransference, when reflected on carefully, can offer valuable insight into the client's emotional state, particularly when the client is disconnected from their own embodied experience.

Ultimately, the therapist's presence – rooted in self-awareness, curiosity, and emotional containment – creates the conditions for clients to explore sexuality not just cognitively, but relationally and somatically. The therapist becomes a witness and companion, not a voyeur or expert. The client, in turn, discovers that their erotic self is not too much to be seen, heard, or understood.

Key Takeaways and Conclusion

Sexuality is a vital and dynamic part of human life, yet it remains one of the most underexplored dimensions in psychotherapy. When therapists neglect to ask about sex – or avoid it due to discomfort – clients may silently carry shame, confusion, or unmet needs that remain untouched by the therapeutic process. Conversely, when sexuality is integrated as a legitimate and meaningful topic, it can open pathways to greater healing, authenticity, and connection.

As this chapter has shown, sexual issues rarely exist in isolation. They are often embedded within the broader context of a client's history of attachment, trauma, cultural identity, relational dynamics, and bodily experience. Addressing them requires more than technique. It calls for depth, presence, and a commitment to complexity.

Therapists working with sexual material must draw from multiple frameworks: behavioral sex therapy for skill-building and structure; relational and attachment-based models for understanding intimacy and conflict; trauma-informed and somatic approaches to reestablish safety in the body; and culturally responsive perspectives to unpack the sociopolitical contexts that shape erotic life. This integrative stance not only reflects the reality of clinical practice, but also honors the many ways in which sexuality intersects with who we are and how we heal.

Some of the most profound therapeutic moments happen when clients dare to say something they have never spoken aloud – when they give language to a fantasy, a fear, a desire, or a wound. These moments require a therapist who can remain attuned and grounded, who does not flinch in the face of taboo, and who can hold space for the unknown. As Esther Perel reminds us, "The quality of our relationships determines the quality of our lives." And the quality of our sexual lives – so often considered separate – is central to this equation.

To support this kind of work, therapists must engage in their own ongoing learning and unlearning. This includes seeking supervision or consultation, engaging with the literature on sexuality and eroticism, attending trainings that challenge implicit biases, and practicing the very emotional regulation we ask of our clients. As therapists deepen their comfort and clarity, they become not just clinicians, but cultural translators – able to help clients make sense of internal conflicts, renegotiate outdated scripts, and reclaim parts of themselves that were once silenced.

In short, to talk about sex in therapy is not a departure from the therapeutic task, but rather it is the work. It is an invitation into the heart of human vulnerability and vitality. And it is a call to listen – not just to what is said, but to what has long been left unsaid.

Summary of Key Principles

- **Sexuality is intrinsic to psychological well-being.** Therapists must be prepared to include sexual concerns in the scope of therapeutic inquiry, regardless of whether a client presents with a sexual problem.
- **Effective sex therapy is integrative.** It draws on behavioral, psychodynamic, somatic, trauma-informed, and culturally sensitive frameworks to address the layered complexity of erotic life.
- **Client concerns about sex often mask deeper issues.** These include shame, relational trauma, attachment wounds, and identity conflicts. Therapists must be willing to go beneath the surface.
- **Therapist self-awareness is essential.** Discomfort with sexual material can hinder the therapeutic process. Ongoing supervision, training, and self-reflection support growth in this area.

- **Cultural context matters.** Race, religion, gender, class, and technology all shape sexual identity and behavior. Therapists must explore these influences with humility and openness.
- **Safety, consent, and pacing are foundational.** Especially in the aftermath of trauma, the therapeutic relationship must model what healthy, attuned connection can feel like.
- **Sex therapy is not about fixing dysfunction.** It's about fostering integration, curiosity, and a more compassionate relationship to one's own body, desires, and relational patterns.

For Clinical Reflection

- How comfortable am I initiating conversations about sex in therapy, even when clients do not explicitly raise the topic?
- What personal experiences, cultural messages, or training gaps shape my beliefs about sexuality – and how might these influence my clinical work?
- In what ways do I notice my own body and emotional responses when clients speak about sexual material? What might these reactions be telling me?
- Do I have a supervision or consultation space where I can process countertransference and explore my own growth areas around sexuality?
- How do I respond when a client's sexual beliefs, practices, or fantasies differ from my own? Can I hold space for curiosity and complexity without rushing to interpretation or correction?
- What training or reading might support me in building greater fluency around attachment, trauma, somatics, or cultural dimensions of sex therapy?
- Can I model an affirming and non-pathologizing stance toward sexuality in the way I ask, listen, and reflect – so that clients feel invited, not exposed?

Chapter 2

Listening to What We Feel
Countertransference as Compass

When people talk about sex – particularly when there are problems with sex – they bring a complex array of emotions to the conversation. There is frustration, anger, disappointment, loss, fear, confusion, anxiety, disgust, shame, humiliation, jealousy, and a profound sense of vulnerability. At the same time, there can also be difficulty in allowing for the more affirmative feelings that sex can evoke: pleasure, joy, surrender, power, lust, hunger, desire, and arousal. As a therapist, it can be challenging to hold and metabolize all these feelings, especially when we might harbor our own discomfort around sexuality.

Psychoanalytic training has traditionally emphasized the therapist's mind – how we interpret, contain, and analyze the unconscious. But far less attention is given to the therapist's body. This absence is especially striking in sex therapy, where the work is not only verbal but deeply somatic. The therapist's body, like the client's, is not passive. It listens. It reacts. It tightens, softens, heats up, pulls away. It often knows something before the mind does. These physical responses are not distractions. They are data, especially in the realm of sexuality, where much of what is felt cannot yet be said.

The Body Speaks First: Countertransference and Embodied Listening

As clinicians, we face a unique challenge addressing sexuality in the therapeutic setting. Historically, therapy training programs have provided minimal focus on sex and sexuality, leaving many clinicians without much knowledge, practical experience, or education on how to manage sexual material or navigate their own countertransference. Because societal, cultural, religious, personal, and familial shame often operate unconsciously in conversations about sex, this terrain is fertile ground for therapeutic projection, avoidance, and enactment.

DOI: 10.4324/9781003318187-3

Yet these complexities offer a rich opportunity. Engaging thoughtfully with sexual content allows us not only to help our clients explore their own embodied histories, but to attend to what is stirred in us. The therapist's affective and somatic responses – our countertransference – are not simply noise to be managed; they are essential clinical tools.

In this work, the body often speaks before the mind. Somatic counter-transference refers to the therapist's embodied responses – often subtle and unconscious – that mirror or resonate with the client's unspoken material. A sudden heaviness in the chest while hearing about a client's shutdown, a feeling of numbness during a dissociated narrative, or unexpected erotic charge in response to a client's fantasy – these sensations carry meaning. They may reflect the client's own internal state, or they may point to dissociated affect held in the therapeutic field. As theorists like Dori Laub and Thomas Ogden have noted, what cannot yet be verbalized often emerges in the form of bodily experience.

Here is a clinical example: I remember sitting with a client who described her sexual experiences with her husband as "fine" and "normal." But as she spoke, I was aware of a flatness to her description, and I noticed a dull ache settle in my chest. It wasn't pain exactly, but a sense of wanting more. Her words were flat, but my body felt hungry. That contrast became a clinical clue. When I gently reflected it back – "As you talk, I feel a kind of ache, like something's missing" – her eyes welled up. "That's exactly it," she said. "I don't feel anything anymore. I've gone completely numb, yet I also feel like I'm starving." My body had heard her truth before her words could name it.

Exploring Sexual History

Often, it is this kind of embodied noticing that leads us into deeper layers of the client's story – including their earliest experiences of sexuality and relational meaning. One of the first questions I ask clients about their sexual history is, "What is your earliest memory of sexuality?" This is an interesting question to ask ourselves too.

I vividly recall the first day of my sex therapy training group. The facilitator invited us to reflect on why we were interested in this work and what we hoped to gain from the experience. I had a polished, professional response prepared: I was seeing more couples struggling with sex, and it felt like the natural next step in my development. But beneath that answer was something more charged – a kind of rebellious excitement at the prospect of talking openly about sex, and a persistent, uneasy awareness that I too felt self-conscious and anxious about this task. I wondered whether I could speak about sexuality so freely without becoming overwhelmed with emotion. I thought about the silence in my family of origin around talking about emotions in general. And the complicated history I had with my own sexual development. This experience mirrored the very ambivalence and vulnerability our clients bring into the room.

Most clinicians enter the field with the implicit belief that professionalism means neutrality. But in sex therapy, neutrality is complicated. We each have a sexual history, a body that remembers, and a set of beliefs and anxieties – many of which formed long before we ever entered a consulting room.

My early discomfort in sex therapy training wasn't simply about the topic – it was about exposure. To talk about sex clinically meant confronting the parts of myself that still held shame or uncertainty. I noticed how easily I could speak with intellectual authority, and how difficult it was to feel emotionally settled when the material touched something personal. My body would respond: a tightness in my neck, a sudden heat in my face, a tensing of my shoulders. This wasn't a sign I was unprepared to do the work. It was a reminder that I was *in* the work.

Adrienne Harris (1996) has written powerfully about how our subjectivity as therapists is never singular. Instead, we operate through multiple self-states – some conscious, others less so – that are activated in different relational contexts. In this way, the therapist's own history becomes part of the analytic field. As Philip Bromberg (1998) suggests, the therapist's ability to "stand in the spaces" between self-states – without collapsing into defensiveness or dissociation – is what allows genuine relational contact to occur.

Therapists who work with sexuality are not immune to the cultural shame, trauma, and repression that saturate our clients' experiences. We are shaped by the same societal messages. Our strength lies not in our ability to transcend this, but in our willingness to stay in relationship with it. To sit within the discomfort. To reflect on where we tense up, shut down, or over-identify. To ask: What part of me is activated or present right now? And what part of the client – or their history – might that be resonating with?

Owning our vulnerability does not diminish our professionalism. It deepens it. When we are attuned to our internal multiplicity, we can meet our clients not as perfect observers, but as fellow humans navigating the complexity of erotic life.

With the right therapeutic environment, the release of pent-up emotion and trauma is possible, and a deeper, more embodied healing can happen. Contemporary trauma research confirms what many clinicians have long observed: traumatic experiences become stored in the body, and sexuality is often the landscape where these somatic memories are enacted. Sexual symptoms, which often show up as avoidance, compulsivity, dysfunction, or dissociation, can be understood as unconscious bodily communications about earlier experiences that have not been fully integrated.

For many clients, having the experience of talking about and reflecting on their sexual development is incredibly therapeutic and insightful in and of itself. Suzanne Iasenza, a pioneer in the sex therapy world, recommends taking an extensive sexual history of each individual and couple. The data collected in these sessions provides valuable information on how a variety of factors have contributed to a person's sexual development. Examples of these questions include:

- What did you learn about relationships and sexuality from your family of origin?
- What was your parents' relationship like?
- How was affection shown in your family?
- How was nudity/body image handled?
- What were the spoken or unspoken messages about sex?
- What were your first sexual feelings, your experience with masturbation, with peer sexual play?
- Were there any unpleasant, disturbing, or confusing sexual experiences?
- Any sexual, physical, emotional abuse or neglect?

With these questions, we begin to see that our sexual blueprint emerges much earlier than we might imagine and that our relational experience with our family of origin and early caregivers is an instrumental thread in the tapestry of our sexuality.

As relationship and intimacy expert Esther Perel says, "Tell me how you were loved and I will tell you how you make love."

These histories shape not only our clients' internal templates, but also the emotional and somatic material that shows up in the therapy room, often through the vehicle of countertransference.

Theoretical Foundations of Somatic Countertransference

The concept of countertransference has undergone significant evolution since its original formulation. Freud initially regarded countertransference as the therapist's unconscious resistance – a contamination of analytic neutrality that needed to be minimized. But contemporary psychoanalytic models, particularly within the relational and intersubjective traditions, have reframed countertransference as a valuable diagnostic tool. Rather than obscuring the work, the therapist's responses – when observed with curiosity and accountability – become portals into unconscious material that may not yet be available to the client.

In cases involving sex and sexuality, somatic countertransference is especially significant. Wilma Bucci's multiple code theory (1997) offers a useful framework here. She describes how human experience is encoded across three interrelated systems: verbal-symbolic, nonverbal-symbolic (e.g., imagery), and subsymbolic (e.g., bodily sensation). While much of therapy operates in the verbal-symbolic domain, subsymbolic experience is often the first and deepest register of affective life – especially in early attachment trauma and unintegrated sexual experience. In this model, bodily sensation is not peripheral but central to meaning-making.

Pat Ogden (2006), a pioneer of somatic psychotherapy, extends this idea into trauma-informed work. She emphasizes that therapists must develop somatic awareness not only to understand clients' dissociation and arousal patterns but also to track their own nervous system responses. These responses often reveal what the client cannot yet say. A therapist's sudden depletion in energy, for instance, may correspond to the client's freeze response; a spike of heat or anxiety might indicate unresolved shame or affective spillover in the therapeutic field.

Allan Schore's work on right-brain-to-right-brain attunement also underscores the primacy of nonverbal communication. He argues that therapist–client interaction is regulated as much through implicit bodily cues – tone of voice, posture, eye contact, breathing patterns – as through words. In this frame, somatic countertransference becomes an essential medium through which co-regulation, rupture, and repair occur.

These theoretical models converge on a powerful insight: the therapist's body is not neutral. It is a resonant, responsive field – one that holds echoes of the client's unconscious world. In sex therapy, where dissociation, shame, and arousal are often deeply entangled, the therapist's somatic awareness can reveal patterns of avoidance, repetition, or yearning that may not yet be symbolized. Attending to these cues does not mean acting on them; it means listening with humility, curiosity, and care. What emerges theoretically comes alive in the therapy room, where the therapist's body often becomes the first instrument of insight.

Clinical Application: Using the Body to Understand the Client

When the Therapist's Body Knows First

Sometimes, the most profound clinical insights come not through interpretation, but through sensation. I remember working with a man in his late 30s who had a history of sexual compulsivity and frequent anonymous hookups. In session, he spoke confidently and rationally about his behavior, listing reasons for his choices and even referencing articles he'd read about the psychology of non-monogamy.

As he spoke, I felt a surge of heat rise from my chest into my neck and chin, followed by a wave of dizziness. Though I was seated, the room felt ungrounded, and I had to work to stay alert and emotionally present. This wasn't anxiety; it felt more like dissociation – a kind of numbing spaciousness, as if I were watching myself from across the room. I noticed my breathing had slowed and my hands were cold. The sensation repeated itself across several sessions, becoming familiar and insistent.

Rather than pushing it away, I became curious about the experience. I tracked the shifts in my body and began to wonder if what I was feeling might reflect something in the relational field. After about a month, I took the risk of naming it. I said, "I'm noticing that I'm having a hard time staying fully here right now – almost like something's pulling me out of the present moment. I wonder if that might be happening for you, too?"

His face changed, and he took a deep breath. "When I talk about sex, I feel like I talk about what I want, but not necessarily what I feel. It's a little like I go into another world." From there, we began to explore a somatic disconnection he had never named before.

As we followed that thread, he began recalling early experiences – moments in his teenage years when masturbation became a way to escape from insecurity and frustration. What had once seemed like a behavioral issue now revealed itself as a nuanced pattern of detachment: an erotic ritual rooted in dissociation, not desire.

So often, the body senses the fracture long before the mind is able to name it.

Erotic Charge and the Boundaries of Attunement

In another case, I worked with a woman in her 40s who was navigating a new sexual awakening after leaving an emotionally repressive marriage. Our sessions were rich with energy and vitality. She often spoke with intensity and described fantasies she had never shared with anyone. I noticed that I felt energized, intrigued, and excited. And while the sessions felt enjoyable and fun, I also paid close attention to these feelings.

I asked myself: Was this my own excitement about her newfound freedom and liberation? Was I mirroring her arousal, or unconsciously taking up the role of a validating other she never had? I didn't disclose these exact sensations to her, but I used them to inform the pace and tone of the work. I slowed my voice a little. I stayed grounded. I paid close attention to whether the energy in the room was moving toward connection, titillation, or dissociation.

Eventually, she said, "I've never felt so safe being this honest about sex." The boundary wasn't just maintained, it was what made the intimacy possible. My ability to stay with her, fully present in body and mind, helped create the safety she had never experienced in sexual relationships.

And sometimes, countertransference speaks not in the moment, but in the spaces between sessions.

Countertransference Beyond the Session

Countertransference experiences can arise in a variety of ways. Sometimes, these experiences are immediate and accessible – you feel a flutter of attraction, a sudden muscle twitch, a wave of sadness or fear. These responses might emerge while a client is speaking about a sexual encounter, describing a traumatic event, or even sitting in prolonged silence. In these moments, the therapist's emotional and bodily reactions often mirror something of the client's internal world. When understood with care, they become a direct portal to unconscious meaning.

At times, these sensations are relatively easy to decipher. A client who recounts feeling rejected may evoke feelings of longing or abandonment in the therapist. A description of aggressive sex might provoke discomfort or excitement, depending on the therapist's own sexual history or boundaries. In such cases, we can name the experience in the room and get curious about why might this be happening right now. What does this tell us about what the client is holding, and how it's landing in the relational field?

Other times, countertransference shows up outside of the consulting room. A client appears in a dream, or we find ourselves preoccupied with them during unrelated moments. We might fantasize about rescuing a client, feel unusually irritable before sessions, or have flashes of memory or emotion that don't "belong" to us in any obvious way. These indirect forms of countertransference can be harder to recognize, but they are no less valuable. They may represent unconscious enactments, dissociated parts of the client's narrative, or affective residue still working its way through us.

Keeping a journal – whether brief session notes, emotional reflections, or dream fragments – can help therapists track these subtle but meaningful experiences. Just as we ask our clients to stay present to the implicit, it's helpful for therapists to do the same. Supervision, consultation, and reflective dialogue offer essential containers for metabolizing this material. As we bring our reactions into language, they begin to transform. What was once a vague discomfort becomes a door into greater insight.

When approached with creativity and curiosity, countertransference becomes not just a mirror of the client's psyche, but a tool for the therapist's own growth and evolution. In the dynamic terrain of sex therapy, where arousal, shame, fear, and longing coexist, this work offers a profound opportunity for both healing and transformation.

Countertransference as a Tool for Healing

In psychoanalytic work and especially with sexual material, countertransference is not a complication to be managed or minimized. It is an essential guide. Our emotional and somatic reactions, if we are willing to study them, can help us understand what the client cannot yet say. They offer a mirror, a container, and often a clue to dissociated or repressed material seeking expression.

Historically, countertransference was viewed as an interference – something the therapist should strive to eliminate in order to remain "objective." But contemporary psychoanalysis, particularly within relational and intersubjective schools, views the therapist's responses as a co-created phenomenon that can provide essential information about the unconscious dynamics in the room. When sexual themes arise, these dynamics intensify. Arousal, shame, anxiety, disgust, or even boredom in the therapist may point toward the emotional residue of the client's early experiences, transferred and enacted in subtle, embodied ways.

Christopher Bollas, in his exploration of the "unthought known," reminds us that there are truths we carry in the body long before they reach conscious awareness. In sex therapy, this is especially resonant. Many clients are trying to speak experiences that were never given language. The body holds these silences, and so does the room and the therapist's body becomes one of the most sensitive instruments for tuning into what remains unsaid.

The embodied therapist listens not only with the mind, but with the breath, with posture, with the subtle currents of arousal and fatigue. This kind of listening allows us to recognize when a client's flat affect masks a deeper erotic yearning, or when a therapist's dissociation mirrors a client's own shutdown. In these moments, our task is not to "get rid of" our responses, but to approach them with compassionate inquiry. What is being evoked in me? What might this feeling represent? What story is the body trying to tell?

Therapists working with sexual material must develop what Pat Ogden calls a "dual awareness" – the ability to remain present with the client while simultaneously tracking one's own inner experience. This capacity to self-monitor allows us to remain in contact without acting out or retreating. When we allow ourselves to feel, and to reflect on those feelings, we deepen our capacity to attune and to respond with thoughtfulness and precision.

The courage to stay in relationship with our internal experience, especially when it feels messy or charged, is part of the therapist's discipline. Naming these reactions, exploring them in supervision, and returning to the therapeutic space with renewed clarity is not just a matter of professional responsibility, it is the heart of psychoanalytic sex therapy. It is how we model curiosity, presence, and nonjudgment.

Final Reflections: The Therapist's Courage

To work with sexuality in therapy is to enter a field charged with projection, history, fantasy, and shame. It asks much of the therapist – not only clinical skill, but emotional courage. It requires that we stay present with what is difficult, awkward, provocative, or painful, and that we do so with humility, containment, and care.

Countertransference, especially in sexual material, is rarely tidy. It can evoke discomfort, arousal, helplessness, or even aversion. But when we turn toward these reactions with curiosity rather than shame, we expand our capacity to accompany clients into the most vulnerable parts of themselves. We offer not just insight, but an experience of being met, seen, and validated without judgment.

This work is not about mastery. It is about presence. It is about listening deeply, with both mind and body, and allowing what emerges in the therapeutic space to guide us. When we honor our own complexity as clinicians, we create space for our clients to do the same. In this way, countertransference becomes not a distraction, but a compass that points us toward what matters most.

Summary of Key Concepts

- **Countertransference is not interference – it is guidance.** Especially in sex therapy, countertransference offers essential information about unconscious dynamics and unsymbolized affect.
- **The therapist's body is a clinical instrument.** Somatic countertransference – tightness, arousal, fatigue, dissociation – can reflect the client's inner world before it becomes conscious or verbal.
- **Somatic awareness supports depth.** Drawing on theories from Bucci, Ogden, and Schore, bodily responses are understood as part of a subsymbolic communication system that precedes language and narrative.
- **Erotic countertransference deserves thoughtful attention.** Rather than being feared or avoided, it can provide valuable insight into power, vulnerability, and the erotic field when handled with clear boundaries and supervision.
- **Multiplicity is the norm, not the exception.** Therapists hold multiple self-states, histories, and vulnerabilities that may be activated in the consulting room. Attending to these with curiosity enhances the therapeutic process.
- **Supervision and self-reflection are essential.** Countertransference – especially when experienced outside the room in dreams, fantasies, or emotional residue – should be explored in consultation and through journaling, not pathologized.

For Clinical Reflection

- How do you experience your body during sessions that include sexual content? What shifts in sensation, affect, or attention do you notice?
- Are there moments when you've felt erotically charged, numb, disconnected, or overly activated? How have you made sense of those experiences?
- What do you understand about your own sexual history, shame, or embodied responses – and how might that shape your therapeutic presence?
- How do you navigate supervision when the material feels vulnerable or personal? Are there places where you avoid bringing certain topics?
- What would it mean to treat your own body as a source of clinical data – not to be acted upon, but to be listened to with care?

Chapter 3

The Erotic Mirror

Narcissism, Trauma, and the Sexual Self

The Grip of Narcissism

The intersection of narcissism and sexuality offers fertile ground for psychoanalytic inquiry. While often cast in pathological terms, narcissism is, at its core, a developmental phenomenon. It refers not to vanity or grandiosity per se, but to the psychic structures that support self-regulation, self-esteem, and relational engagement (Kernberg, 1975; Kohut, 1971). From a developmental perspective, narcissistic defenses arise when early caregivers fail to provide attuned mirroring or consistent emotional regulation. The result is a fragile self that must develop compensatory strategies – idealization, devaluation, perfectionism, emotional withdrawal – to manage vulnerability and protect against psychic fragmentation.

These defenses do not stay confined to the realm of self-image; they infiltrate relational life, especially in the intimate realm of sexuality. Erotic experiences may become rigidly scripted, emotionally disconnected, compulsively pursued, or entirely avoided. Some clients, like Jon, experience arousal only through fantasies that evoke humiliation or secrecy – echoes of developmental environments in which natural curiosity was shamed and affection was conditional. Others might struggle to sustain desire in long-term relationships where mutual vulnerability is required.

Contemporary psychoanalytic thinkers, including Nancy McWilliams (2011) and Philip Bromberg (2006), have emphasized the dissociative underpinnings of narcissistic functioning. The self is not unified but fragmented, with certain affects or experiences split off from conscious awareness. Sexuality becomes one domain where this dissociation vividly plays out. Erotic symptoms – compulsivity, inhibition, lack of desire, or problematic fantasies often represent exiled aspects of the self-seeking expression.

In clinical practice, this dissociation is often experienced somatically through embodied disconnection, numbness, or hyperarousal in sexual contexts. These symptoms are not random but reflect the nervous system's adaptation to environments in which the erotic was unsafe, misattuned, or

DOI: 10.4324/9781003318187-4

shaming. Borrowing from Pat Ogden's work on somatic psychology and Stephen Porges's polyvagal theory, we can begin to understand how the erotic body becomes a container of memory, registering safety or danger in ways that are often preverbal. Healing, then, requires more than cognitive insight. It requires the restoration of regulation and connection through embodied attunement and affective presence in the therapeutic relationship.

Crucially, narcissistic defenses are not chosen; they are adaptive. They emerge in relational contexts where the child's needs for validation, soothing, and autonomy go unmet or are punished. Rather than pathologizing these defenses, the therapeutic task is to understand their logic, to decipher how they helped the client survive, and how they may now inhibit growth.

Positive Narcissism and Early Development

While much attention in both popular culture and clinical literature is devoted to pathological narcissism, it is equally important to understand the role of healthy narcissism in psychological development. When adequately supported, narcissism reflects a cohesive sense of self, a feeling of aliveness in one's body, and the capacity to engage in emotionally and erotically intimate relationships. This foundational sense of worth and self-regard, what Kohut (1971) might call the "narcissistic selfobject function," arises from early relational experiences of attunement, mirroring, and regulation.

From the earliest stages of life, the infant relies on caregivers to regulate affect, provide safety, and offer consistent responsiveness. In the context of "good-enough" caregiving (Winnicott, 1965), the infant internalizes the expectation that their emotional and physical needs will be met. This early attachment security becomes the bedrock for positive narcissism – the ability to trust one's desirability, tolerate vulnerability, and express desire without fear of annihilation or humiliation. In this state, sexuality can be playful, embodied, and mutual.

Theoretical contributions from Hyman Spotnitz (1961), particularly within the framework of Modern Psychoanalysis, provide a useful elaboration of how narcissistic dynamics evolve from preverbal emotional states. Spotnitz viewed narcissistic pathology as originating in early nonverbal trauma, where unmet needs for recognition and soothing left the developing ego without adequate tools for verbal expression and relational mutuality. He emphasized the importance of working with narcissistic transference as a means of reaching affective states that predate language and are often expressed through body symptoms, acting out, or primitive defense mechanisms.

From this perspective, erotic development is deeply tied to how early rage and longing were handled or mishandled by caregivers. The erotic body, in this view, holds memory traces of both the ecstatic pleasure of connection and the searing pain of misattunement. If early rage was disavowed or met with rejection, erotic energy might become cut off, dissociated, or diverted into fantasy, symptom, or control. Spotnitz's concept of the therapist using their own countertransference as a "treatment tool" is especially relevant in sex therapy, where unspoken sexual material often manifests through shifts in the therapist's body, mood, or fantasy life.

Healthy narcissism allows for a felt sense of worth and erotic entitlement – that is, the belief that one deserves pleasure, connection, and attuned touch. When these early developmental processes unfold in a holding environment that tolerates frustration and delight alike, individuals develop the capacity to surrender, to be seen, and to experience erotic joy in the presence of another.

But when these early needs go unmet – when soothing is inconsistent, attunement is absent, or vulnerability is met with shame, defensive narcissism may take root. In such cases, sexuality can become performative, compulsive, or emotionally disconnected. The body becomes a site of both yearning and defense. As we will see in the next section, these dynamics often emerge vividly in sexual fantasies and behaviors that initially appear puzzling or even disturbing, but which, when explored with care, offer a portal into the client's earliest relational world.

Narcissism and the Erotic Body

Sexuality often becomes the terrain where narcissistic patterns are vividly enacted. Erotic symptoms, whether they take the form of avoidance, compulsivity, inhibition or fetishes, can function as unconscious messages from the body. These expressions are not random; they emerge from the architecture of the self, shaped by early developmental experiences and encoded in somatic memory. In this sense, the erotic body becomes both stage and actor, telling stories that the conscious mind may not yet be ready to articulate.

Joyce McDougall (1986) described fantasy as a "theater of the body," where dissociated parts of the self come to life symbolically through arousal and desire. Sexual behavior may carry traces of early injuries – moments of humiliation, secrecy, or loss of agency – reenacted not literally, but symbolically. The symptom, then, is not just a dysfunction to be corrected, but a doorway into meaning.

Psychoanalyst Phyllis Meadow (1995a), in her work on the erotic body, understood sexuality as a complex interaction between preoedipal trauma and the ego's effort to organize experience. For Meadow, the erotic symptom serves not merely as a neurotic compromise but as a creative construction of the self, formed in response to unbearable internal states. Rather than eliminating the symptom, Meadow encourages therapists to listen to its structure – to uncover how the fantasy stabilizes identity, mediates shame, and provides access to dissociated affect. The erotic body, in her view, speaks its own language: one that requires patience, precision, and poetic interpretation.

Similarly, Hyman Spotnitz's (1961) insights on narcissistic transference offer valuable clinical guidance when working with sexual material. Spotnitz emphasized how preverbal and unformulated affect often manifests through bodily symptoms or projective processes, especially in narcissistic patients who lack the internal structures for verbal symbolization. In sexual functioning, this can appear as somatic distress, compulsive enactments, or fragmentation of erotic identity. Spotnitz reminds us that our job as therapists is not only to interpret but to regulate – to serve as a containing object for affect states that could not be held early in life. This is particularly relevant when sexual desire is infused with rage, shame, or helplessness.

When sexuality becomes a site of dissociation, the therapist's body may function as a sensitive barometer of the unspoken. Somatic countertransference, such as tightness in the chest, changes in breath, sudden fatigue, or agitation, can offer subtle but powerful clues about what remains disowned in the client's narrative. As Pat Ogden and Janina Fisher have shown in their somatic work with trauma, the body often registers what the mind cannot yet name. In these moments, the therapist's embodied awareness becomes not a distraction, but a clinical instrument – illuminating dissociated affect, psychic conflict, or unmetabolized erotic charge that the client may not yet be able to verbalize.

Clients may enter therapy with profound shame about their arousal patterns – particularly when their fantasies are rooted in taboo, humiliation, or secrecy. The question is not whether a fantasy is "healthy" or "appropriate," but what emotional truth it carries. Sexual fantasy, like dreamwork, reflects an internal logic, even if it defies conventional understanding. What does this fantasy allow the client to feel? What intolerable affect might it be managing? What early relational themes does it attempt to repair or repeat?

These fantasies, while often laden with shame, can be crucial symbolic vehicles through which the client attempts to metabolize early trauma. Clinically, it becomes essential to discern whether the fantasy is operating as a compulsion – a reenactment of earlier powerlessness – or as a reparative experience that reclaims agency and self-definition. This differentiation often rests not in the fantasy content itself but in the emotional and relational context surrounding it. Are the desires engaged with consciously and playfully, or compulsively and secretly? Is there room for integration and dialogue, or only dissociation and hiding? These questions guide the therapist in supporting the movement from unconscious repetition toward conscious re-symbolization.

The following case brings these theoretical themes to life through the story of Jon, a man whose erotic life illustrates the complex interplay between dissociated shame, early relational trauma, and symbolic sexual expression. His experience demonstrates how narcissistic defenses can become encoded in sexual fantasy and functioning – and how, when met with attunement and curiosity in therapy, these symptoms can transform into portals for integration, embodied healing, and renewed relational presence.

Case Study: Jon

Jon, a heterosexual man in his early 30s, sought individual therapy to address sex-related issues with his girlfriend. He had recently begun having difficulty maintaining an erection during sex and wanted to understand why. Though generally content in his relationship, he described his girlfriend as critical, feeling he never quite met her expectations.

His family history revealed parents who placed high expectations on their children to excel academically and follow their medical careers. Jon was a compliant child eager for parental approval. He excelled in school, attending a prestigious college and earning a PhD in a science-related field.

During the sexual functioning assessment, Jon reported difficulty feeling sexual toward his girlfriend yet continued their "normal" weekly sex, which increasingly felt obligatory. When asked about masturbation, he became notably avoidant. He reluctantly admitted to masturbating several times weekly but grew nervous when asked about masturbation fantasies.

As a psychoanalyst, I might have respected his resistance. However, sex therapy tends to be more direct. My compromise was acknowledging his discomfort while inquiring about its source. Jon responded that he had never discussed masturbation and wasn't sure why it mattered.

I recognized this as resistance to exploring deeper meanings in his sexuality – what I call an "Anxiety/Shame spot." When exploring sexual functioning, certain questions trigger discomfort, typically by touching on shame. The response is anxiety that can induce similar feelings in the therapist, who might question the validity of exploring sexual issues: "My patient's sex life is none of my business," "I'm being voyeuristic," "Why do I need specific details," "I should respect privacy."

As psychoanalysts, we know that countertransference feelings often represent projections of the client's emotions. The more comfortable we are tolerating these feelings and demonstrating ease in discussing sex, the easier it becomes for clients to integrate their sexual feelings. With sex-related issues, the therapist often needs to take the lead – different from general psychoanalytic psychotherapy where one typically waits for the client to introduce material. Sex therapy often requires the therapist to introduce language, normalize sexual experiences, and provide education.

After this uncomfortable session, Jon canceled two appointments. When he returned, he requested using the couch (which he had previously resisted). The couch can help manage shame by reducing embarrassment from face-to-face interaction. I inquired about his missed sessions and their possible connection to the last session and masturbation discussion. He acknowledged discomfort, saying masturbation seemed private and unrelated to his sexual functioning. He was embarrassed to share his masturbation fantasy.

Jon reluctantly revealed always masturbating to golden shower fantasies (being urinated on). He laughed nervously, apologizing for being "sick." As he spoke, I noticed a tightening in my muscles and an overall feeling of being tense – a familiar signal for me that unspoken shame is present. I had learned to track these micro-responses in my own body not as distractions, but as part of the dialogue. They often told me what the client could not yet say. He didn't connect this masturbation practice to his erection problems during "normal" sex and thought he should simply stop masturbating to this fantasy. He continued to apologize profusely for this fantasy and suggested we should just stick with talking about his erection problems, wondering whether Viagra would be an easy and appropriate fix. At that moment, I noticed my own internal reaction: I was feeling self-conscious, wondering if I was pushing Jon to talk about something too uncomfortable. I could sense my own anxiety. I took a few internal breaths and focused on calming down my own anxiety. In slowing down the pace, I began to wonder what my reaction was about. Was this a subjective reaction to Jon's material or to the vulnerability in the room? Was it my discomfort or his that I was experiencing? It really didn't matter, but I felt it important for me not to shy away from the discomfort. Acknowledging the awkwardness of the moment, I said "I know how uncomfortable this can be to talk about and I get your interest in finding a solution to the erection problems. I'd like to just stay with this for a moment because the discomfort could be relevant and I want to understand this better. There is no need to apologize because fantasies are often rooted in taboo themes. I don't have any judgement related to your fantasy – only an interest in better understanding it and seeing if there might be a connection to your erection problems with your girlfriend. It seems like you have two different variations to how you are sexual, one in the privacy of masturbation and fantasy and the other when you are sexual with your girlfriend."

I recognized Jon's strong avoidance of unpacking and discussing his fantasy. I acknowledged his discomfort but emphasized the need to explore potential connections between his "private" fantasy and "normal" sex. It's helpful for therapists to monitor countertransference reactions that might collude with topic avoidance, especially around shame, humiliation, or disgust. Important questions to inquire about are: When did this fantasy begin? When did you start masturbating to it? When did you begin keeping it secret? In what ways might this fantasy connect to childhood experiences?

I noted that this aspect of Jon's sexuality wasn't relational – he couldn't integrate the fantasy into sex with his girlfriend, and it was accompanied by considerable discomfort and shame. The privacy surrounding the fantasy seemed significant, as did his reluctance to speak about it openly. Where there is shame, there is often narcissistic vulnerability. It appeared more like a self-protective attachment to a specific erotic experience – one that functioned as a closed loop, excluding mutuality. Jon's reluctance to verbalize his fantasy also resonated with what Adrienne Harris describes as the multiplicity of self-states – where erotic experience can become compartmentalized, unformulated, or split off from relational engagement.

In psychoanalytic terms, sexual symptoms can reflect an unconscious narcissistic transference onto the body, where unmet developmental needs become lodged in somatic experience. As Bessel van der Kolk (2014) writes in *The Body Keeps the Score*, trauma often leaves its imprint not just on the mind but on the body itself. Jon's struggle to speak about the fantasy – and the embodied discomfort that accompanied it – signaled to me that the fantasy itself might be holding deeper emotional meaning.

Stephen Snyder (2018), a contemporary sex therapist, describes such impasses as "erotic knots": intrapsychic or relational tangles that constrict sexual vitality. These knots can't be untied through insight alone; they require curiosity, symbolic exploration, and the slow work of relational attunement. It's essential not only to explore the fantasy itself, but also to widen the scope – inviting inquiry into how early family dynamics may be woven into the erotic fabric.

As the therapy progressed with Jon and I continued to normalize taboo sexual fantasies without judgment, his discomfort and shame lessened and he was able to reflect and share more openly about both his fantasy and the development of his sexual interests.

Jon was the youngest child with two older sisters. As a child, he was curious about watching his mother and sisters urinate. His mother often left the bathroom door open when urinating, and he would watch, asking about differences between how boys and girls urinate. Despite being a physician, his mother dismissed his natural curiosity with simplistic answers about anatomy.

Jon vividly remembered his sisters urinating in their shared bathroom. They teased him for sitting rather than standing to urinate. He described the teasing as playful rather than mean, though it left him feeling embarrassed and somewhat humiliated alongside their affection.

Jon described feeling excited by "access" to his mother's and sisters' private world of urination. Early on, he experienced keeping this "secret" and would pretend disinterest while secretly paying close attention. This evolved into interest in smelling their worn underwear, which he would take from the hamper, enjoying the smell and taste. During adolescence, he masturbated while smelling the undergarments.

Once his mother caught him masturbating with her soiled underwear and was appalled: "Why are you doing this? What have I done to you that would make you do this?" Jon apologized profusely, remembering vividly the humiliation and shame. This incident linked shame with arousal. Though he continued the behavior, he felt ashamed afterward.

After exploring his childhood and adolescent history, we discussed how his fantasy affected current sexual functioning. He found it secretly arousing when women used the bathroom, with masturbation fantasies of being caught watching women urinate. In his fantasy, they would be appalled at his voyeurism and punish him with golden showers. The humiliation of getting caught and subsequent punishment was highly arousing. Some fantasies included being forced to clean women's vulvas, being used as "toilet paper," resulting in the woman having an orgasm on his face – a kind of forced cunnilingus.

After masturbation, he experienced little embarrassment and could detach from shame. It motivated him to have "regular sex" with his girlfriend – standard intercourse involving kissing, fondling, and penetration. But this "regular sex" was disconnected from authentic desire or arousal; it was his obligation or duty. His authentic desire remained secret. He saw satisfying his girlfriend as his job – which he enjoyed enough (similar to pleasing his parents in childhood). This sexual split worked until erection problems brought him to treatment, where intense shame and humiliation surfaced through discussing his fantasy.

In subsequent therapy, Jon repeatedly apologized for his "sick" fantasy. Over several months, we normalized his experience, examining how his fantasy might have originated from natural childhood curiosity about bodies and sexuality. We considered how his fantasy connected with experiences of affectionate teasing, embarrassment, and later humiliation and shame. As a child always doing the "right thing" by meeting parental expectations around success and achievement, it made sense that doing the "wrong thing" could be simultaneously shameful and arousing.

In sex therapy, it's important to provide clients space to explore these themes without necessarily making sense of everything or reaching conclusions. Tolerating the "not knowing" in sexuality allows for curiosity and playfulness – precursors to sexual pleasure. It also frees people from attaching sexual experience to particular outcomes like erections or orgasms.

As Jon began understanding his fantasy's potential origins and meaning, his apologizing decreased. However, he became increasingly concerned with quantifying "acceptable" fantasy engagement: Would weekly masturbation be okay or excessive? Monthly? Or should he stop entirely?

I avoided direct answers and explored his ambivalence. We examined the division between "masturbation" and "regular sex" and how this split kept his desire dissociated from relational sex. Jon had never considered that sex with another person could feel exciting and arousing. Though uncomfortable sharing his fantasies with his girlfriend, he wondered if there was a way to make sex with her feel more authentic and arousing.

Through collaboration, we experimented with reducing masturbation frequency and allowing himself to become aroused by golden shower fantasies before having sex. He began initiating sex with his girlfriend (instead of masturbating) when aroused by the fantasy. This breakthrough allowed him to experience more spontaneous and natural arousal in partnered sex. As he grew comfortable discussing his sexual fantasies, he became more comfortable owning his desires and initiating more satisfying sex that incorporated his fantasy.

We then expanded his sexual repertoire – in sex therapy, this is called "developing/expanding the sex menu." People often have narrow scripts around what constitutes sexual experience, and expanding the menu explores and broadens their sexual repertoire. Oral sex became a new feature of Jon's sexual menu – a more "normal" act he felt comfortable experimenting with. While performing oral sex, he could still focus on a woman's vulva and vagina, incorporating the arousal from image, scent, and taste. He enjoyed the intimacy of oral sex, which maintained elements of "private access" to female sexuality. But instead of a solo experience, he expanded the fantasy to incorporate feeling connected to his arousal during partnered sex.

I suggested Ian Kerner's book *She Comes First* – a manual for performing oral sex on women – and the website *OMGYes*, which features instructional videos on female pleasure, oral sex techniques, and female masturbation. Jon found this website arousing, informative, and affirming. Oral sex became a satisfying addition to his sexual repertoire with his girlfriend. His masturbation became less compulsive and decreased in frequency (his goal), and his erection problems resolved.

Eventually, Jon and his girlfriend ended their relationship due to fundamental compatibility issues. He later met a sexually adventurous woman with whom he felt more naturally connected. She had a "kinky side" she was comfortable with, and for the first time, Jon shared his fantasies with someone outside therapy.

Jon's movement from compulsive secrecy to relational disclosure reflects a shift from enactment to engagement – from a defensive erotic script to a shared one. In Mitchell's (2002) language, sexuality becomes less about control or avoidance and more about mutual meaning-making. The shift is not merely behavioral but symbolic: the fantasy becomes integrated rather than isolated, offering new affective territory where Jon can be both desiring and desired.

Jon's case brings to life many of the theoretical themes introduced earlier in the chapter. His sexual symptoms were not simply dysfunctions to be corrected, but embodied expressions of deeper intrapsychic conflict, shaped by early attachment wounds and carried forward through dissociated fantasy and shame. Drawing on object relations theory, we can understand his fantasy life as a symbolic language through which unmet needs for connection, affirmation, and recognition were being expressed.

Jessica Benjamin's work on mutual recognition and intersubjectivity provides a compelling lens through which to understand Jon's struggle. At the heart of narcissistic injury is not only the failure to be mirrored, but the loss of relational subjectivity – the terror of being truly seen by another. Benjamin (1995) notes that healthy development requires the oscillation between self-assertion and surrender, between being recognized and recognizing the other. In Jon's case, the surrender of control was only tolerable in fantasy, and even then, it had to be embedded in humiliation and secrecy. Partnered sex with his girlfriend demanded a kind of mutual vulnerability he had no template for. His arousal could emerge only when dissociated from intimacy – where he remained unseen, anonymous, controlled. His therapy involved not only unpacking the fantasy, but slowly building the capacity to stay present with his own desire in the presence of another. His masturbation fantasy served both as a defensive structure – protecting him from relational vulnerability – and as a covert attempt at regulation, echoing what Phyllis Meadow described as a narcissistic transference to the erotic body. Similarly, Joyce McDougall's concept of fantasy as a "theater of the body" helps frame his internal erotic life as a stage where unintegrated parts of self could emerge. Through the therapeutic relationship, Jon was gradually able to bring these split-off experiences into conscious awareness, reclaiming them as part of a more integrated, embodied sexual self. His journey underscores how psychoanalytic sex therapy can transform not only behavior, but identity and meaning, allowing clients to access greater authenticity, pleasure, and relational presence.

Jon's therapeutic arc highlights the power of an integrated psychoanalytic and sex therapy framework – one that does not pathologize fantasy or reduce erotic expression to symptom, but rather listens closely to the unconscious messages embedded within sexual material. His case demonstrates how the erotic can become both a mirror and a portal: reflecting long-standing relational patterns, while also opening the possibility for new modes of connection, regulation, and vitality. The therapeutic process did not require Jon to "fix" his fantasy, but rather to understand and reclaim it – transforming it from a source of shameful secrecy into a relationally viable dimension of his erotic identity. In doing so, the work helped loosen the rigid defenses of narcissism, allowing for greater authenticity and mutuality. These themes invite us to reconsider the clinical role of sexuality – not as peripheral to identity, but as central to the unfolding of a more cohesive and integrated self.

At its core, Jon's journey was not only about fantasy integration, but about reclaiming the right to be known. As Benjamin suggests, recognition is more than acknowledgment – it is the co-creation of subjectivity. In allowing his fantasy to be seen without shame, Jon entered a new relational paradigm: one where his erotic life no longer had to be hidden, but could serve as a bridge to deeper intimacy.

Integrating Narcissism and Sexuality in Clinical Practice

Jon's case illustrates the complex interplay between narcissism and sexuality that clinicians frequently encounter. At the root of his sexual difficulties was a narcissistic split – a division between his authentic, embodied desires and his performative, relational sexuality. This split originated in early developmental experiences in which natural curiosity and sensuality became entangled with shame, secrecy, and humiliation. The resulting pattern exemplifies how narcissistic defenses can become embedded in sexual functioning, often manifesting as compartmentalization, inhibition, or compulsivity.

From a psychoanalytic perspective, symptoms like Jon's are not just behavioral problems to be corrected, but signifiers of internal conflict – clues to dissociated or disavowed aspects of the self. The sexual symptom becomes a symbolic expression of unmet needs and unconscious fantasy. Working psychoanalytically means attending to these meanings while also holding the body and its responses as central to the therapeutic process. In Jon's case, his arousal template was organized around a traumatic fusion of humiliation and affection. This fusion shaped not only his fantasy life but also his difficulty accessing desire in relational sex, where vulnerability and mutuality required the very trust his early experiences eroded.

Therapeutic work involved not only surfacing Jon's unconscious fantasy life but also creating the safety, attunement, and pacing necessary to metabolize shame. As Meadow (2003) suggests, the erotic body is often the last repository of the dissociated self – the final frontier for self-recognition and healing. What was once split off in service of survival becomes available for integration through a therapeutic relationship that can tolerate ambivalence, contradiction, and the unknown. Hyman Spotnitz's focus on preoedipal dynamics and the therapist's emotional communication also offers a relevant frame: Jon's relational shift occurred not only through interpretation but also through a process of emotional holding that mirrored a more secure early attachment experience.

This integrative process also included elements of contemporary sex therapy, such as psychoeducation, behavioral experimentation, and developing a broader sexual script. These practical tools supported Jon's efforts to reconnect with desire in the presence of another – transforming what had been a solitary, shame-bound experience into one that could include intimacy, curiosity, and co-constructed pleasure. Adrienne Harris (2005) offers another valuable framework through her emphasis on the multiplicity of self-states and the role of affect regulation in identity formation. From this perspective, Jon's erotic life can be understood as a fragmented expression of split-off parts – self-states that were never held or metabolized within relational space. His shame-bound desire operated in isolation, cordoned off from the relational self that performed adequacy and compliance. Harris reminds us that the therapeutic task is not to unify the self into a cohesive whole but to create the conditions under which dissociated states can come into contact, be held in language, and eventually be regulated. Jon's work in therapy wasn't just about disclosure – it was about tolerating the friction between competing parts of himself: the ashamed boy, the compliant partner, the aroused voyeur, the curious adolescent, the anxious adult. Therapy became the space where those parts could coexist without collapse or moral panic.

The relationship between narcissism and sexuality is bidirectional: early narcissistic wounds shape our sexual expression, while our sexual experiences either reinforce or challenge our core self-structures. A client's arousal patterns may become rigid, repetitive, or dissociated in ways that reflect a history of emotional neglect, unmet mirroring needs, or traumatic intrusions. At the same time, as clients begin to experiment with new ways of relating sexually, they may also shift internalized beliefs about their worth, lovability, and relational potential. This reciprocal process opens a path toward reorganization – not only of sexual function but of self-concept.

Perhaps most importantly, this approach acknowledges both the wounds and the possibilities embedded in narcissism and erotic life. Jon's story reminds us that sexuality is not only a function to be restored – it is a portal to deeper integration. Through curiosity, containment, and a willingness to explore taboo or shame-bound territory, therapy can help clients reclaim dissociated aspects of the self and build a new relationship with their desire. This work is often slow, nonlinear, and emotionally charged. But when successful, it allows the erotic to become a site not only of anxiety or secrecy, but of vitality and connection.

Summary of Key Concepts

- **Narcissistic defenses often emerge from early relational trauma** and can profoundly shape sexual functioning, fantasy life, and relational patterns in adulthood.
- **Healthy narcissism is foundational to erotic vitality** – it supports the capacity for mutuality, surrender, and embodied pleasure. When disrupted, sexuality may become disconnected from intimacy or constrained by rigid scripts.

- The erotic body can hold dissociated aspects of self, particularly those tied to shame, humiliation, or unmet developmental needs. Symptoms may carry symbolic meaning that reflects deeper unconscious processes.
- Sexual fantasies are not pathologies to be fixed but narratives to be explored. Understanding the emotional truth beneath fantasy can facilitate integration and relational authenticity.
- Psychoanalytic sex therapy provides a rich framework for addressing the complex intersections of narcissism, trauma, and sexuality – drawing on relational theory, somatic awareness, and unconscious meaning.
- Clinical work requires tolerance for ambiguity and shame, as well as the therapist's attunement to both verbal and nonverbal communication, especially in highly charged erotic material.
- Healing involves moving from dissociation to connection – from secrecy and performance toward authenticity, curiosity, and pleasure shared in relationship.
- Mutual recognition supports healing: When therapists hold erotic material without judgment, clients can move from shame-bound secrecy toward relational subjectivity and emotional freedom.

For Clinical Reflection

- In what ways have you encountered narcissistic defenses playing out in your clients' sexual expression or fantasy life? How do you distinguish between protection and pathology?
- How do you track your own somatic countertransference when working with shame-bound or taboo erotic material? What signals emerge in your body?
- When a client's fantasy evokes discomfort, curiosity, or judgment in you, how do you metabolize those reactions in service of the work?
- How do you navigate the tension between validating a client's erotic truth and exploring the potential unconscious meanings embedded within it?

Chapter 4

Power At Play
BDSM, Relational Dynamics, and Therapeutic Healing

Introduction: Theoretical Framework

The intersection of power, sexuality, and relational dynamics presents a rich and often misunderstood terrain for psychological exploration. Within the realm of BDSM – bondage, discipline, sadism, and masochism – clients engage with themes of control, surrender, intensity, and transgression in ways that can be deeply meaningful. Contemporary psychoanalytic theory has evolved significantly in its approach to these practices, shifting away from pathologizing assumptions toward recognizing kink and BDSM as potential sites of emotional truth, attachment healing, and erotic vitality.

At the heart of BDSM is a paradox: the voluntary relinquishment of power can yield a deeper sense of agency, authenticity, and connection. Jessica Benjamin's work on intersubjectivity offers a powerful lens for understanding this dynamic. Rather than reinforcing binaries of "doer and done to," BDSM – when consensual and collaborative – can create a space for mutual recognition, where each partner holds the other's subjectivity while engaging in clearly defined roles. Benjamin (1988) argues that healthy domination and submission require the capacity to sustain relational tension without collapsing into control or compliance. This capacity is central to reparative kink practices.

Jack Morin's (1995) concept of the "erotic equation" further expands this perspective. He suggests that our erotic preferences are shaped by early emotional experiences – particularly those charged with tension, taboo, and ambivalence. The ingredients of what he calls our "core erotic theme" often emerge from moments in which vulnerability and excitement were interwoven. Morin invites us to see desire not as pathology but as a map of unresolved emotional meanings – ones that can be explored and transformed through fantasy, play, and conscious embodiment.

From a clinical standpoint, BDSM may replay early relational wounds, but it also offers the possibility for revision. David Ortmann and Richard Sprott (2013) argue that BDSM, far from being symptomatic of

DOI: 10.4324/9781003318187-5

dysfunction, can be a powerful expression of agency, healing, and resilience – particularly for those with complex trauma histories. Within the clear boundaries of negotiated roles and scenes, clients may reclaim dissociated parts of themselves, reenact prior experiences with new outcomes, or access a sense of control over previously overwhelming emotional states.

Margaret Nichols (2020) emphasizes that clinicians must adopt a sex-positive, trauma-informed lens when working with kink-identified clients. She advocates for a model that centers consent, non-pathologization, and curiosity about the meanings embedded in erotic behavior. Nichols argues that the clinician's comfort level – both with the content and the emotional resonances of BDSM – plays a critical role in creating a therapeutic space where clients can safely explore and integrate these experiences.

As such, the goal is not to interpret BDSM practices as evidence of dysfunction but to explore what the client is attempting to express, resolve, or integrate. For some, submission may offer relief from hypervigilance; for others, dominance may provide a corrective experience of being heard, obeyed, or valued. The therapeutic task is to help clients discern whether their participation in BDSM reflects reenactment of trauma, avoidance of vulnerability, or a conscious movement toward erotic and emotional integration.

When practiced consensually and with attunement, BDSM can become a powerful site of both pleasure and transformation. It can allow for the reclamation of bodily agency, the expression of long-silenced desires, and the renegotiation of power in a way that fosters mutual care. This chapter explores these possibilities through the lens of Brian's story – a client whose journey through kink, heartbreak, and discovery illustrates how erotic authenticity and emotional safety can coexist, and even catalyze profound healing.

The therapeutic task when working with BDSM material is not to pathologize the erotic but to remain curious about its deeper emotional logic. Rather than rushing to normalize or interpret, we begin by listening – allowing the erotic to speak in its own language of sensation, symbolism, and affect. As sex therapists and psychoanalysts, we're often called upon to hold space for fantasies that carry layers of meaning and memory, often rooted in preverbal or shame-bound experience. In this context, our role is to help clients metabolize these erotic expressions not as anomalies to be corrected, but as coded messages from the unconscious, rich with relational significance.

For some clients, the experience of consensual submission or domination is not simply a sexual preference – it's an emotional necessity. These scenes can offer a symbolic structure through which unresolved powerlessness or invisibility can be re-scripted into felt experiences of trust, containment, and mutuality. But the line between reenacting past trauma and transforming it is often subtle and subjective. This is where clinical discernment and a strong therapeutic alliance are essential.

Brian's story offers a vivid illustration of this complexity. His exploration of spanking fantasies and BDSM encounters emerged not in a vacuum, but within the emotional debris of a long-term, contemptuous relationship and the psychic residues of childhood shame. Through the therapeutic process, these fantasies became more than isolated arousals – they evolved into symbolic enactments of trust, containment, and relational repair. His case highlights how BDSM dynamics can surface in therapy not only as clinical challenges, but as portals into deeper integration. What follows is a clinical narrative that brings these concepts to life, illuminating how erotic authenticity and emotional safety can coexist – and how kink can become a site for transformation rather than reenactment.

As clinicians, it is vital to distinguish reenactment from reparative experience – not by their outward appearance, but by their underlying structure. Reenactments are often marked by compulsive repetition, dissociation, and a lack of reflective capacity. In contrast, reparative experiences arise when erotic play is grounded in consent and agency. These encounters can allow clients to revisit sites of trauma with new internal and relational resources, transforming scenes of shame or helplessness into moments of vitality and self-recognition. This distinction is not always obvious from the outside, which is why our clinical curiosity – and attunement to affective tone and meaning – becomes so essential. What follows is a clinical case that brings this distinction to life.

Brian's Journey

Brian sat in my office reminiscing about his scene last week with Roger. He had a glow about him as he described the intensity of Roger's spankings – the sting of firm slaps against his bottom as a room full of onlookers watched. He spoke of the pride he felt at his endurance, taking one hard spanking after another. He described the embarrassment and shame of being exposed to a room full of other gay men, characterizing this combination as an erotic cocktail that would later fuel his orgasm.

It was after these scenes that Brian felt most enamored with Roger, grateful to have found a partner who perfectly matched his kinky erotic template.

This moment of fulfillment contrasted sharply with Brian's earlier therapy sessions. Not long ago, he sat in my office feeling beaten down and hopeless, struggling to untangle himself from the belittling relationship dynamic that overshadowed his marriage to Edward. Divorce was something he had never anticipated and certainly hadn't actively wanted. Yet as we explored the problems in his marriage, it became increasingly difficult for Brian to stay. He experienced excruciating pain as awareness grew of how profoundly unhappy he was.

Brian and Edward had been together for 15 years. Brian described their marriage as difficult, and he entered therapy to address their emotional and sexual rift. It had been several years since they had sex together, and although Brian had other sexual partners through their open relationship agreement, he felt beaten down and burdened. The companionship and support they once shared had faded, replaced with criticism, judgment, and contempt. Edward was dismissive and mocking of Brian's newfound interest in BDSM, calling him names and ridiculing his attendance at BDSM parties and experimentation with impact play. Brian had tried to include Edward, suggesting he accompany him to a party and explaining the excitement he experienced when acting out his submissive fantasies. But week after week, Brian sat in my office feeling rejected and defeated as he recounted Edward's cruel words about his spanking fantasy.

During one particularly pivotal session, Brian summarized his disappointment and anger:

> I wish I had never told Edward about going to the spanking party. We have an open relationship agreement, and it's not like I was breaking a boundary. But I thought it might create a spark between us. I was hoping it might turn Edward on and he would be curious or interested in my fantasies. Instead, he won't let it go and uses it to taunt and humiliate me. It's such a painful feeling, to be laughed at. Now Edward uses it against me, blaming me for the lack of sex between us by saying that my "perversions" have made me selfish and uninterested in him.
>
> The truth is that all Edward ever wanted me to do sexually was give him a blow job and service his sexual needs. It got boring, and over time I built up resentment. Because of our open relationship agreement, I didn't feel guilty – I assumed he was hooking up when he needed to. I didn't like how he assumed our sex life was satisfying. I tried talking with him about adding novelty and diversity to how we had sex. His response was that I could experiment outside our relationship, that he was happy with our sexual dynamic. He also dismissed the idea of couples therapy, saying we didn't have any major problems.
>
> So I retreated, silently at first. I just stopped initiating sex between us, and Edward didn't seem to notice or mind. I hadn't been very active with our open relationship agreement, and work was keeping me busy, so instead of trying to hook up with someone, I started masturbating more regularly. I found myself thinking about submissive fantasies, particularly getting a bare bottom spanking. There was something about not being in control that was a turn-on for me.
>
> I had all kinds of fantasies involving being spanked. In these fantasies, I would initially protest out of shyness or embarrassment. But

the man would have a dominant personality and instruct me otherwise. Something about my reluctance, the embarrassment of getting spanked, and feeling like I had no other choice but to accept it was incredibly sexy for me. I repeated this fantasy over and over. I searched out porn that would replicate it, and there was plenty. But my preference was to use my own fantasy. I looked forward to evenings when Edward would be out so I could relax and enjoy masturbating to this fantasy. I would sometimes use a brush to spank myself as I replayed it in my mind.

In my relationship with Edward, I had been mostly deferential to his sexual interests. I'm a people pleaser at heart, so accommodating his turn-ons was fun in the beginning and came naturally to me. Although Edward describes himself as vanilla, he has a dominant side to his personality. He liked the feeling of being serviced sexually. Receiving an extended blow job was his primary way of getting off. I would masturbate myself while giving him head, and I liked to synchronize my orgasm with his. There was something about being in unison with Edward that turned me on. Thinking about it now, maybe it was a way for me to relinquish control and follow his lead. Maybe I've had submissive tendencies all along and didn't even realize it.

Psychoanalysis teaches the skill of following a client's lead, sometimes called "the contact function." Done right, this intervention allows for free association. Remarkable discoveries can happen when we're given the opportunity to wander with our thoughts and speak without direction or clarity. Knowing when to lead and when to follow differs for each client. Brian had a lot to say and was used to being talked over. So I smiled gently, my presence showing curiosity and my quietness giving permission for him to continue. What struck me was how quickly his pain gave way to self-blame. He had learned early that his longings were a liability – and even now, he was trying to package them neatly before revealing them.

At this moment, Brian began to tear up. "What is coming up for you now?" I asked.

"I have tried so hard with Edward. It has been so difficult to feel like he respects me, listens to me, even likes me. He is either emotionally unapproachable or dismissive. It feels like a prison I can't escape from. I'm beginning to realize how much effort I put into trying to connect with him. I accommodate him in so many ways. It's exhausting. Yet in his defense, he doesn't directly ask me to do this. But his personality demands it. You either go along with Edward's program or he finds fault in you. And it's the finding fault that has worn me down. His unwillingness to talk about our relationship or acknowledge there might be a problem leaves me feeling trapped and defeated. I can't do it any longer."

Brian released considerable emotion during this session, allowing himself to feel the sadness and frustration that had built up for years. Toward the end, I asked what it was like to release so much emotion.

"It feels good to get it all out. I feel lighter in some ways, and it helps confirm the problems between us. Another part of me feels confused about moving forward. Edward is so unwilling to talk about these things, yet I don't feel ready to leave. The idea of ending our marriage and being on my own is scary to me."

I reassured Brian that he didn't need to have everything figured out. It was enough that he was processing his feelings and had an outlet to explore his relationship.

Childhood Patterns and Present Dynamics

Over the following months, Brian and I explored the origins of his submissive fantasies and the emotional residue they carried. Our work focused not only on his current relational pain, but on long-standing feelings of inadequacy and shame that seemed to echo through much of his life.

Brian often described feeling "not good enough" – a theme that had shadowed him since childhood. His mother was a strict and emotionally distant woman who maintained high standards for behavior, cleanliness, and academic achievement. Brian, a sensitive and imaginative child, frequently fell short of her expectations. He learned early to mask his inner world and perform compliance. Though he was outwardly polite and well-behaved, inside he felt watched, judged, and not quite right.

His father, though less overtly critical, was absent and disengaged. A workaholic by temperament, he often returned home late and withdrew into television or household tasks. Brian recalled feeling invisible in his father's presence, as though there was no space for his inner life or developing selfhood. Loneliness, he said, was his most enduring childhood memory.

As a young boy growing up in a conservative Midwestern suburb, Brian also carried the weight of being different. Though he wouldn't name his gay identity until later adolescence, he had early experiences of being emotionally and socially out of step with his peers. His interest in fantasy, aesthetics, and relational nuance often set him apart. He described feeling like he had to work harder than others to be liked, accepted, or seen.

In therapy, Brian began connecting these childhood dynamics with the emotional atmosphere of his marriage to Edward. "It's not just that Edward mocks me," he reflected one session. "It's that I shrink when he does it. I feel like I'm twelve again, trying to hold it together so I don't get in trouble. And the worst part is – I keep doing it. I try harder to please him instead of standing up for myself."

This insight marked a turning point. Brian began to understand that his deference to Edward was not just about adult compromise – it was an echo of an older emotional pattern: the anxious striving of a child hoping to earn love through submission, perfection, or emotional containment. He had tried, in both childhood and adulthood, to be easy to love by erasing his own complexity.

What emerged with growing clarity was that Brian's submissive sexual fantasies were not pathological or regressive. Rather, they were encoded with meaning. They were attempts – symbolic, embodied, and creative – to metabolize earlier experiences of powerlessness and shame. His desire to be spanked, dominated, or "forced" into erotic surrender was not a replication of trauma but an attempt to rework it. The fantasy offered an alternative relational template: one in which shame and exposure might coexist with desire and acceptance.

At this point in therapy, Brian had begun exploring his submissive desires in real life through play parties and scenes within the BDSM community. These experiences offered him a liberating contrast to the shame and criticism he endured in his marriage. Yet much of his exploration remained emotionally compartmentalized – intensely arousing but disconnected from deeper relational meaning. He had not yet met someone with whom these desires could be explored in a context of emotional attunement and mutual care. What therapy provided was the space to begin integrating his erotic life with his emotional history – to understand that his fantasies were not something to be hidden or apologized for, but rather windows into long-buried needs for recognition, surrender, and safe containment. This growing insight set the stage for what was to come: an encounter that would shift not only how Brian experienced sex, but how he understood intimacy itself.

Finding Healing Through Consensual Power Exchange

Several weeks later, Brian arrived at his session flushed with excitement and eager to talk.

"I had the most intense and erotic spanking scene last week with a man I find incredibly attractive and sexy. But the best part wasn't the sex – it was the conversation between us and how thoughtful and kind he was to me."

"Roger approached me earlier in the evening and introduced himself. He mentioned that he had noticed me at a few events over the months and found me sexy. He identified himself as dominant and said he particularly enjoyed giving spankings. He gathered from the scenes he saw me participate in that I also had a strong connection to getting spanked and asked if I might want to play with him. He had such confidence as he looked me directly in the eye with a charming smile and joked, 'I promise I will be gentle with you unless, of course, you need to be strongly disciplined?' I could feel the warmth in my cheeks as I blushed deeply, and my body tingled with nervousness and excitement. I laughed a little, trying to think of a witty response, but nothing came to mind. I had this moment of frustration with myself. I was on the verge of spiraling into self-attack and anxiety when he said, 'All flirting and joking aside, if you're interested, let's make sure you have a safe word. I don't intend to do anything too intense, but I do like to push edges. I get the sense that we vibrate on the same sexual level, and I'm pretty certain you would have a great time.' At this point, I was smiling ear to ear and feeling more relaxed. I teased him back, 'Well, I do like to be coerced a little – that's part of the turn-on for me.'"

Brian continued to describe this initial interaction with Roger with delight. They flirted playfully and talked for several hours before agreeing to engage in the spanking scene. I reflected back how pleasurable and intense this exchange seemed for him. He smiled and nodded, saying, "The most powerful part is how kind and thoughtful Roger is. He didn't try to rush, push, or control me. For someone who is sexually dominant, he was so gentle with me. He wasn't domineering in his personality at all, just confident and deliberate. I couldn't help but compare him to Edward and notice how different their personalities are."

In moments like these, I also track my own bodily responses – what somatic psychotherapists call *somatic countertransference*. Do I feel tension, breathlessness, warmth, or contraction? These cues often signal affective material the client may not yet be able to name. When working with intense erotic content, especially involving power dynamics, the therapist's body becomes part of the listening field. Awareness of these internal shifts – when held reflectively – can enhance our attunement and help metabolize unconscious communication that moves through sensation rather than speech. I felt an eagerness and excitement for Brian, as Roger seemed so respectful and loving toward him. I also noticed a rebellious sense of defiance that I was feeling toward Edward. These were internally noticed on my part, almost unconsciously because of how quickly I was responding to Brian's emotions.

"How would you describe their differences?" I asked.

"Edward is simply mean. He doesn't respect me, and his behavior makes that apparent. But he's not even willing to admit to that. He has all this judgment and contempt toward my sexual interests that he brushes off as his 'opinion.' It comes across as so dismissive. He is truly sadistic without admitting to it. Why would you treat someone you supposedly love with such contempt and cruelty?

Roger, on the other hand, is so kind and loving toward me. He seems to enjoy who I am as a person and treats me with acceptance and respect.

He is curious about me and values my opinion. He is everything I always wanted in a partner but was never really able to articulate to myself."

This mutuality exemplifies Jessica Benjamin's (1995) concept of "mutual recognition," where both partners experience themselves and each other as full subjects. For Brian, who had long submitted to contempt and ridicule in his marriage, Roger's dominance offered something entirely different – not control for its own sake, but a co-created space in which Brian's needs, limits, and desires were actively held. The intersubjective recognition of his submissive self, without ridicule or rejection, enabled Brian to reclaim a part of his erotic identity once split off by shame.

Brian's recounting offered a clear example of what some theorists describe as reparative enactment – a consciously engaged, embodied experience that allows the client to transform earlier trauma within the container of negotiated play. Unlike the dismissive contempt he experienced with Edward, Roger's attunement created space for Brian's submissive desires to be explored without shame. This contrast wasn't incidental – it was central to Brian's healing.

As Brian allowed himself to inhabit the submissive role with Roger, his nervous system also began to revise its implicit memory of dominance and exposure. Borrowing from Stephen Porges's (2011) polyvagal theory, we can understand this shift through the lens of neuroception – the body's capacity to detect safety or danger beneath conscious awareness. In earlier relational contexts, submission had been equated with humiliation. But in the presence of Roger's attunement, Brian's system registered safety, allowing a reorganization of meaning. As Pat Ogden and Janina Fisher (2009) argue, therapeutic healing often requires not only cognitive reframing but also somatic reprocessing – where the body registers "a different ending" to an old story.

As clinicians, we must learn to differentiate between repetition compulsion and reparative encounter. In the former, clients unconsciously replay trauma in a way that reinforces old wounds, often without awareness or agency. These reenactments may feel urgent, familiar, or compulsive – but they rarely lead to integration or healing. In contrast, reparative experiences are marked by choice, safety, and the presence of an attuned other. When the conditions of consent, mutuality, and containment are in place, clients can re-enter emotionally charged territory not to repeat the past, but to re-script it. In this light, Brian's engagement with Roger was not a retraumatization, but a reclamation – an opportunity to author a new narrative in which his submissive desires were met with curiosity, care, and erotic attunement. He was not simply acting out old wounds but transforming them through embodied enactment in a context of dignity and relational presence.

Psychoanalytic theory reminds us that transformation does not always arise through verbal insight or interpretive clarity. It often unfolds through embodied experience, especially in realms like sexuality where language may fail to capture affective complexity. Sometimes healing comes through the body's memory and the felt sense of difference – what Pat Ogden might describe as *somatic reprocessing*, and Stephen Porges would call the *neuroception of safety*. In Brian's case, his autonomic nervous system began to revise old associations: submission no longer signaled humiliation, but connection; exposure no longer triggered shame, but aliveness. Through Roger's attuned dominance, Brian's internal working model of intimacy began to shift. His fantasy life – once fragmented and somewhat unknown – began to integrate with his relational life. The "scene" with Roger was not merely sexual role play; it was a moment of psychic synthesis, in which previously disowned aspects of self came into contact with care and recognition.

This encounter also exemplified Jessica Benjamin's influential notion of mutual recognition – a relational space in which both people are experienced as full subjects, capable of influencing and being influenced. In such dynamics, dominance and submission lose their hierarchical valence and become relational roles imbued with responsiveness and care. Roger's dominance was not coercive or controlling in the traditional sense; rather, it was a deliberate erotic stance, performed within boundaries that protected both his and Brian's subjectivity. Within the BDSM frame, Brian could access emotional vulnerability without collapsing into shame. He could inhabit his arousal without losing self-respect. This capacity – to hold intensity and tenderness together – had long eluded him in other relational contexts. Now, within the safety of this new encounter, it was finally becoming possible.

"What's even more amazing is that he can move into this sexual domain where he takes total control. I can trust him because I know he respects me as a person, and that makes it feel safe. I can let myself feel 'bad or naughty' and surrender to his dominance because I know it's safe – he doesn't really think I am bad, even though in those moments I feel embarrassment and shame."

"Instead of the fear and anger I feel with Edward, I feel excitement with Roger. We are playing with power, and it's an edgy and powerful experience. He lets me go to the darker parts of my personality in this way that feels intense – a little scary but also safe. These sexual experiences feel like they tap into a deep emotional well and create a lot of sexual energy. I've never had such intense orgasms before, and the sexual energy lasts beyond the initial scene. I can remember a scene and masturbate to it for days and even weeks later."

"There is an exhilaration I feel that spills over into my whole life and an appreciation and love for Roger that just keeps deepening. He allows me to feel vulnerable in a way that isn't shaming. Something that I haven't felt with Edward in many years and never before at this level. I feel like I am experiencing a deep sexual and emotional healing."

As Brian spoke these words, I was reminded of how paradoxical BDSM can be – how submission can unlock agency, how dominance can express love, and how erotic power play, when grounded in trust, can become a powerful tool for repair. This was not a contradiction. It was the erotic truth of Brian's story finally coming to light.

Conclusion: Power, Consent, and Relational Healing

Brian's story invites us to reflect on the deep relational meaning embedded within consensual BDSM practices. Far from pathological, his submission became a vehicle for reclaiming agency, integrating desire, and restoring dignity to parts of himself long burdened by shame. Through his encounters with Roger, Brian re-scripted the emotional template laid down in his family of origin and reenacted in his marriage with Edward – not by avoiding his fantasies, but by embodying them within the container of safety, attunement, and mutual recognition.

The work of psychoanalysis has always been to make the unconscious conscious. But in the realm of sexuality – and particularly in BDSM – it is often the body that tells the deeper story. When verbal narratives fall short or become distorted by shame, the body may still remember. What emerges in scenes of negotiated dominance and submission is not merely theatrical role play, but a symbolic language – a ritualized choreography of need, longing, and psychic transformation. These erotic scripts, especially when enacted with care and consent, often surface material that is preverbal, affect-laden, and historically charged. As clinicians, our task is not to stand outside these enactments as detached observers, nor to pathologize them based on normative expectations, but to enter the terrain with curiosity and attunement, helping clients explore how their erotic expressions carry both the residue of trauma and the potential for repair.

This chapter underscores the clinical importance of distinguishing reenactment from reparative experience. While both may involve repetition, the difference lies in the presence – or absence – of agency, containment, and recognition. When the foundational elements of consent, communication, and care are in place, BDSM no longer functions as a compulsion to relive old wounds. Instead, it becomes a revisioning of the past – a deliberate return to emotionally fraught territory, now infused with safety and choice. In this context, submission is not collapse or erasure, and dominance is not aggression or domination in the destructive sense. Rather, these become dynamic roles – intentionally chosen, collaboratively enacted – that offer clients new relational outcomes, fresh somatic possibilities, and expanded meanings for desire. It is in this imaginative and embodied space that integration becomes possible and where the erotic is reclaimed as a source of vitality.

Clinicians must also attend to their own countertransference responses, especially when working with taboo fantasies or power-laden dynamics. Feelings of discomfort, arousal, protectiveness, judgment, or fascination can all serve as valuable clinical data – signposts of where the therapist's unconscious meets the client's material. Rather than viewing these reactions as intrusions, we can understand them as invitations to reflect more deeply on our own assumptions about control, vulnerability, and erotic legitimacy. In supervision and reflective practice, metabolizing these reactions can sharpen our capacity for presence and prevent subtle forms of avoidance, collusion, or moralizing.

In parallel, working with BDSM material also raises ethical considerations, especially around therapist comfort, competence, and bias. Clinicians must avoid conflating personal discomfort with clinical risk. When therapists harbor unexamined judgments or moralizing attitudes, they may inadvertently shame or pathologize clients. Ongoing training, supervision, and consultation – particularly with kink-aware professionals – are essential to provide affirming, competent care.

Above all, Brian's journey reminds us that sexuality is a portal – not just to pleasure, but to deep emotional truth. The therapeutic relationship, when held with integrity, can help clients navigate these portals with courage and clarity, expanding their capacity for intimacy, embodiment, and authentic connection.

Summary of Key Concepts

- **BDSM is not inherently pathological:** When practiced with consent and care, BDSM can offer powerful opportunities for healing, intimacy, and self-integration.
- **Erotic templates are shaped by early experience:** As theorized by Jack Morin, our turn-ons often emerge from the interplay of pleasure, risk, and unresolved emotional themes. These templates can be sites for exploration, not shame.
- **Consent transforms power:** Power dynamics in relationships are inevitable, but when named and negotiated – as they are in BDSM – they can become vehicles for mutual recognition and trust rather than reenactments of trauma.
- **The difference between reenactment and repair matters:** Clients may repeat early relational wounds in sexual behavior. The therapeutic task is to help them differentiate compulsive repetition from reparative experience grounded in agency and mutuality.

- **Embodiment matters:** Somatic experience and nervous system regulation play a crucial role in integrating sexual desire with emotional safety. As Brian's story shows, healing can occur not just through words, but through the body's memory of being met and accepted.
- **Countertransference can be a compass:** Therapists' emotional responses to sexual material may reflect the client's shame, longing, or defenses. Exploring these reactions with supervision and curiosity can enhance therapeutic presence and precision.
- **Sexuality is a portal to the self:** Erotic expression often carries unconscious meaning. When therapists approach this material with curiosity, permission, and respect, they help clients reclaim their right to pleasure and authentic connection.

For Clinical Reflection

- How do you differentiate between a client's reenactment of trauma and a reparative BDSM experience? What cues – verbal, somatic, relational – guide your interpretation?
- In what ways do your own assumptions about power, dominance, submission, or control shape how you hear and respond to clients' BDSM practices?
- What feelings arise in you – curiosity, discomfort, arousal, protectiveness, moral tension – when a client discusses BDSM or taboo fantasies? How do you work with those responses?
- How do you assess for safety, consent, and agency in clients' BDSM experiences without undermining their autonomy or pathologizing their desires?
- When a client's erotic expression seems incomprehensible or extreme, are you able to stay in a posture of clinical curiosity? What helps you hold that space?

Chapter 5

Sexual Healing
Masturbation, Trauma, and the Body's Wisdom

The Body as a Site of Healing

Contemporary trauma theory increasingly positions the body as the primary locus of both injury and recovery. As Bessel van der Kolk (2014) famously writes in *The Body Keeps the Score*, traumatic experience is not simply a memory stored in the mind – it is inscribed in posture, tone, tension, breath, and movement. For survivors of sexual trauma, the very physiological systems responsible for pleasure, arousal, and safety often become dysregulated. Touch may trigger fear; desire may summon shame. In these cases, reclaiming sexuality requires more than insight – it requires re-patterning the body's felt sense of safety, choice, and embodied agency.

Somatic modalities such as Somatic Experiencing (Levine, 1997) and Sensorimotor Psychotherapy (Ogden & Fisher, 2009) emphasize that healing trauma involves restoring the organism's capacity for self-regulation by completing thwarted defensive responses. This includes trembling, vocalizing, pushing, or even masturbating – not as regression, but as integration. The erotic, in this context, is a vehicle for reorganization.

For some clients, masturbation becomes an unlikely but powerful site of this reorganization. Unlike partnered sex, which can stir relational anxieties, solo sexual activity offers an attuned, self-directed space where the survivor can reinhabit their body at their own pace. When approached with curiosity and permission, masturbation can offer a somatic language through which dissociated affect finds voice. It may surface as breath, moan, movement, contraction, or trembling – bodily acts that echo the preverbal registers of early trauma and can serve as portals for emotional release.

In this framework, orgasm is not the goal but the byproduct of a deeper process. As Holly Richmond (2021) argues, embodied pleasure becomes a medium through which new neural pathways are formed – ones that link sexuality not to fear or fragmentation, but to groundedness, vitality, and choice.

DOI: 10.4324/9781003318187-6

Reclaiming Pleasure After Trauma

For many survivors of sexual trauma, reclaiming pleasure is not a linear or purely joyful process – it is a layered, often ambivalent return to the body after years of dissociation and internalized shame. While popular discourse frequently emphasizes sexual empowerment as a destination, in clinical practice we see how pleasure can also provoke fear and grief. Clients may find themselves aroused and overwhelmed simultaneously, or experience orgasm as both catharsis and collapse. To hold this complexity, therapists must create space where embodied pleasure is not reduced to functionality or performance, but explored as an evolving emotional landscape shaped by relational history.

In this context, masturbation becomes not just a means of self-stimulation but a form of exploratory somatic witnessing. When approached with curiosity, solo sexual expression can surface exiled emotions, symbolic enactments, and buried affective memory. The case of Connie illustrates how this private realm of experience – which is often marginalized in clinical dialogue – can offer vital clues to unresolved trauma and unintegrated self-states. Her story invites us into the raw, nonlinear terrain of erotic reclamation.

Clinical Vignette: Connie's Erotic Landscape

"I sometimes get this sexual urge when I am alone in the house. It's a tingling in my body, knowing that I can masturbate without interruption. It's also a feeling of excitement and slight fear, like I am doing something bad, defiant or rebellious. There is a gnawing in my stomach and in my vulva. When I begin to stimulate myself, it feels primal, raw and like an endurance test. There will be overstimulation and discomfort, sort of like getting tickled uncontrollably. I will want it to stop and that's in part what makes it feel good. It's a childlike feeling of excitement and risk, as I give myself permission to indulge in afternoon solo sex. I turn the vibrator on to the highest level and press it firmly against my clit. Strong waves of stimulation pulse through me. The stimulation is almost impossible to take. I have to squeeze my legs together because of the intensity and that dulls the sensation. But the dulling sensation is arousing and then I begin tapping and rubbing the vibrator against me. I wouldn't describe the sensation as painful, but there is definitely overstimulation. I press down harder on the vibrator and push myself into a state of endurance. I make these sounds that I have no idea where they come from. It's a grunting and snorting. It's a growl that comes from deep in my throat. I grit my teeth. I let out loud moans. I push out short breaths. I feel like an animal. Sounds, noises, gestures and movements come out of my body that I would be so embarrassed by if anyone were to see or hear me. It feels raw and primal. It usually only lasts a few minutes. It's all I can tolerate physically. It's a hard and intense orgasm and I usually break out crying afterwards. It's an intense build up and then an intense release. Sometimes I will fall asleep, but mostly I just finish crying and then get on with my day, not giving it much other thought. Except that lately I have begun to wonder why I do this, why it feels so secretive and private and I have a yearning to share the details with someone."

Connie's raw and sensory-rich account reveals more than a masturbation routine – it offers a window into the body's unconscious memory. Her description evokes Peter Levine's (1997) concept of *pendulation* – the rhythmic movement between activation and deactivation in trauma healing. The intense stimulation, muscular clenching, and subsequent release may function as a form of *biological discharge*, allowing Connie's body to process implicit memory that predates language or linear narrative.

The physicality of her masturbation – marked by sounds, movement, and momentary overwhelm – can also be viewed through the lens of *sensorimotor psychotherapy* (Ogden & Fisher, 2009), which emphasizes how trauma is held and expressed somatically. What might appear as overstimulation or intensity could in fact be the body's way of completing self-protective responses that were previously truncated by dissociation. The experience of "being an animal" reflects a return to primal, embodied knowing – what Pat Ogden calls *bottom-up processing*, where sensation leads the therapeutic experience.

When Connie arrived in therapy, she had a specific topic to explore related to her sexuality and masturbation. She described a masturbation process that felt intense and raw to her. She had never talked about it before. She didn't have any conscious shame about it, yet also felt embarrassed by the visceral bodily responses that occurred during masturbation. She wanted to better understand the emotional punch that it had on her and to confront the embarrassment by talking about it.

Clinically, one could theorize that Connie's drive to speak about this private, embodied ritual signals an emerging integration. As psychoanalytic thinkers like Dori Laub and Cathy Caruth have argued, trauma often exists in the unspeakable – what has yet to be translated into language or symbolized within relational space. Connie's yearning "to share the details with someone" can be understood to be not just a disclosure; but rather a developmental moment, a shift from repetition toward narration. In trauma-informed psychoanalytic frameworks, this movement is central to healing: the previously unspeakable becomes sayable, the dissociated becomes integrated. What Connie brings is not just content – it is process. The very act of naming and reflecting on her embodied experience initiates transformation.

Connie was very deliberate about the kind of therapy experience she wanted and had a slow pace in mind. Before beginning to unpack the masturbation experience, she wanted to spend some time talking in general about her experience with therapy and other self-help practices. She felt it important to give some history and context to her therapeutic journey and the positive impact it had on her overall sense of confidence and self-esteem.

Connie was a seasoned veteran of therapy and self-improvement. She described an almost ten-year history with a variety of therapeutic experiences and an ongoing interest in self-development. She read books on self-improvement and attended a variety of coaching, therapy, and spirituality workshops and seminars. Most notably, she had worked very hard to overcome the negative impact of her history of childhood sexual abuse. She felt quite proud of the healing and growth she had experienced through her many years of therapy and the confidence that she had gained in herself. She described having a "settled" feeling – a grounded kind of experience within herself, where she felt aligned with herself and anchored in her body.

This "settled feeling" reflects what somatic and psychodynamic traditions might call embodied integration – a state in which traumatic affect is no longer split off, and the self feels more coherent. Pat Ogden describes this as "earned regulation," where the nervous system no longer cycles between dysregulation and collapse, but instead supports a capacity for presence and agency. Connie's narrative echoes this evolution: from dissociation and performance to grounded self-observation and curiosity about her sexual self.

However, this wasn't always the case for Connie, as she described feeling a sense of detachment for most of her life. She was the girl in childhood who was coined as "being lost in her own thoughts." She was a "thinker" and loved to daydream and drift off into imagination. She went on to study philosophy in college and then eventually became an art therapist specializing in trauma.

This developmental pattern – early dissociation paired with rich internal life – can be viewed through both a neurobiological and psychoanalytic lens. From a polyvagal perspective, Connie's childhood daydreaming might be understood as a dorsal vagal shutdown response, a form of protective withdrawal that supports psychic survival in the face of chronic threat. From a psychoanalytic viewpoint, her deep imaginative world likely served as a transitional space (Winnicott, 1971a), allowing for the preservation of selfhood despite developmental rupture. That she later became a trauma therapist herself is not uncommon; many clinicians arrive to this work through their own history of hurt and healing.

Connie described a history of molestation that occurred intermittently for about ten years of her childhood, ranging from ages 6 to 16. The abuse came from an adult neighbor who was close to their family. Connie would always pretend to be asleep when the abuse was happening. She described her body moving into a frozen state, while her mind would fragment. She experienced her mind floating out of her head while her body remained frozen.

It was through her many years of therapy that she was able to work through the anger and shame that plagued her emotional life. It was also through a variety of different therapy approaches, including trauma work and somatic practices, that she was able to reconnect with her body in a way that felt safe, grounded, and integrated. Her own training and development as an art therapist specializing in trauma also helped pave the way for her continued healing and growth.

Often in the early months of our work together, I invited Connie back to her original interest in discussing her sexuality and masturbation. We hadn't actually begun talking about the specific topic that brought her into therapy with me, although the history that Connie was providing seemed a relevant backdrop. My approach with clients is to let them take the lead, at least in the beginning, to help me better understand their understanding of the issues and to provide an open forum for exploration. I am also mindful of any stated goals they have and make a point of keeping those goals active in our conversations. It's easy to get sidetracked in therapy, and often the veering off topic can yield interesting and significant discoveries. Letting the pull of our unconscious direct us is absolutely a worthwhile endeavor, as is maintaining focus and being deliberate about achieving certain results. I see my role as a therapist in being a guide to both of those paths.

Slowly, we began to talk about Connie's relationship to her sexuality. She described being a sexually aware person and enjoyed sex. She was sexually adventurous in her young adult years and typically ended up with boyfriends with whom she had a strong sexual connection. There was also a way that she historically "held back" from her sexual experiences and didn't feel fully present for them. Sex was somewhat of a performative act for her – an act that she felt good at and enjoyed, but knew nonetheless that there was some detachment there.

This detachment is not uncommon in trauma survivors, especially those whose early experiences involved bodily boundary violations or disempowerment. As theorist Janina Fisher (2017) notes, traumatic disconnection from the body often emerges as a survival response but later becomes a barrier to authentic embodied intimacy. For Connie, sexual enjoyment was possible, but often split off from deeper emotional presence. Her ability to "perform" masked a more vulnerable truth – one of ambivalence, self-protection, and unintegrated arousal. This pattern also aligns with what McDougall (1986) described as the "anti-erotic body," where intense physical sensations are divorced from affective meaning, and sexuality unfolds in a vacuum of disconnection.

In her mid-30s, she began to have a strong desire to have a child and get married. Sexual chemistry was not as important for her when thinking about an ideal partner, but she did end up marrying someone with whom there was initial sexual compatibility. As with many couples, once they had a child, sex became less frequent as their identities as parents became more central in their lives. Connie noticed a significant shift in her husband's personality toward her. He was previously complimentary of Connie's achievements and attributes, but since becoming parents, he often focused on his perceived flaws in her parenting approach. Connie described experiencing a steady flow of complaints and criticisms related to her parenting. It seemed like she could do nothing right in the eyes of her husband.

She couldn't understand the negativity that she felt from her husband, and attempts at parenting or relationship conversations between them quickly turned into heated arguments that were not easily resolved. This created an emotional wedge between them that continued to grow over time. By the time their daughter was 5, they were living parallel lives and effectively co-parenting their daughter, but the emotional bond between them was damaged beyond repair. They divorced two years later.

After her divorce, Connie felt a reconnection to her sexuality. She wasn't ready to commit to another relationship while her daughter was young, but she did develop an ongoing sexual relationship with a man named Dave whom she trusted and cared deeply for. It was also during this time that she began to masturbate with more regularity. She hadn't ever put much thought into her masturbation practice until recently. She was beginning to notice a pattern that she felt had relevance, and was curious to explore. This was the topic that prompted her to seek out therapy again. It was this pattern that she wanted to explore and talk about.

From a clinical standpoint, Connie's newfound interest in solo erotic practice can be viewed as a reparative act. Winnicott's (1960) concept of "creative aloneness" offers a useful framework here: masturbation becomes a transitional space in which the self is neither intruded upon nor abandoned, but free to explore sensation, impulse, and play in the presence of internal safety. For survivors of sexual trauma, this kind of exploratory solitude is often necessary before partnered intimacy can be reestablished on new terms. As such, Connie's growing curiosity about her masturbation can be understood not as a retreat from intimacy but a stepping stone toward integration.

Connie's descriptions of her private erotic rituals – tinged with both fear and freedom – reflect not only a unique coping strategy but also a powerful attempt at self-regulation. Her solitary sexual practice emerged not from a place of pathology, but as a form of *self-holding* in the Winnicottian sense: a transitional space in which she could experiment with feeling without external threat.

From a trauma-informed psychoanalytic perspective, Connie's embodied arousal represented a partial return of the repressed – not just in psychic terms, but as a reawakening of bodily self-agency. Her capacity to experience excitement in her own body without dissociation seemed significant. Here, we see the relevance of Bessel van der Kolk's (2014) assertion that *the body keeps the score*, but we might go further and say: the body also holds the possibility of reclaiming the story.

Masturbation, for Connie, became a medium through which fragments of memory, desire, and grief could be encountered symbolically. Her capacity to articulate the sensations – *a tingling, a wave, intense stimulation* – and the private setting in which they occurred signals a growing ability to metabolize trauma through what Pat Ogden et al. (2006) calls "interoceptive awareness": the mindful tracking of internal states. This somatic self-witnessing offered her a bridge between dissociated sensation and meaningful affect.

Psychoanalytically, Connie's journey also illustrates what Jessica Benjamin (1990, 2004) describes as the movement toward intersubjective recognition – not just in the therapeutic dyad, but within the self. In masturbation, she was no longer a passive object of past violation, but an agent of present pleasure. Through therapy, she began to see herself *seeing* herself – a dual awareness that allowed for both mourning and mastery.

Importantly, Connie did not merely "resume" sexual functioning. Her healing involved re-signifying erotic experience through a process of narrative integration and embodied permission. Cathy Caruth (1996) reminds us that trauma is not only what happens but also what continues to elude understanding. Connie's desire to speak about her erotic ritual was a signal that what had once been unspeakable was now ready to be symbolized – *not fully resolved, but reachable.*

Masturbation as Somatic Reprocessing

Orgasm from masturbation was a very different experience for Connie than anything she experienced during partnered sex. She used a vibrator to masturbate that had a variety of speeds and consistently used the highest setting. She would put the vibrator directly on her clitoris and begin to experience immediate and intense stimulation. She described the experience as an intense mix of pleasure and pain. She would tighten the rest of her body to help tolerate the intense stimulation. She described the experience similar to an endurance test of intense stimulation. She would clench her legs together and begin to make grunt-like sounds, a mixture of short breaths and long wails. Her legs would begin to shake as she felt the build-up of sexual energy, but she continued to clench them together and rock her pelvis in conjunction with the sounds coming out of her mouth. The peak experience would last no longer than a minute or two. Sometimes she would pace herself and start with the vibrator on a lower setting, allowing herself a more prolonged build-up. Other times, she would repeat the process several times, allowing herself several orgasms. Connie's masturbation practice reflects what Pat Ogden et al. (2006) and other somatic trauma theorists describe as a "procedural memory loop" – a repetitive, embodied behavior that encodes not only sensation but affective meaning. Her tightening, clenching, and vocalizing weren't merely physical reflexes; they were patterned responses likely rooted in the body's earlier adaptations to overwhelming experience. In this context, masturbation became more than release – it was a ritual of emotional endurance, of staying present with intensity that might otherwise fragment her. This kind of patterned stimulation – intense, rhythmic, primal – can also be viewed through Peter Levine's (1997) concept of "biological completion," in which trauma recovery involves discharging thwarted survival energy through controlled somatic experience.

What was most interesting to Connie was the emotion that was associated with her masturbation practice. She described making the grunting noises as she would begin with the vibrator and feel a mix of frustration and anger. It wasn't a self-attacking kind of frustration or anger, and the experience didn't feel punishing in any way. She described it as follows:

> It's like there is a build-up of emotion that I am releasing or a deep well of frustration and anger that I am tapping into. The sounds that I make are animal-like; it's a very primal experience. It's embarrassing to say, but I feel like an animal in those moments. It's not anything I would ever show to a partner. It feels too personal and private for me. In those moments, it's like I am growling in both pain and pleasure. I never paid attention to it before, but recently Dave and I have been experimenting with masturbating together, and I noticed how differently I masturbate in front of him. With Dave, I am more focused on pleasure in my masturbation. Masturbating with Dave is fun and erotic. We are both watching each other receive pleasure, and that adds to the erotic charge. It's a voyeuristic pleasure and a physical pleasure. When I masturbate alone, I am tapping into deep feelings and making animalistic sounds. I'm not having any kind of thoughts or fantasies. It feels like a deep body-based experience. In fact, the closest thing I can relate it to would be having contractions and giving birth.

This powerful comparison to birth contractions opens up important clinical territory. As Phyllis Meadow (1995b) has suggested, erotic expressions often function as symbolic enactments of early developmental processes – pain, separation, protest, even emergence. Connie's description positions her solo orgasm as both primal and reparative, a reenactment of embodied intensity that paradoxically makes her feel more present. Her "animalistic" sounds may reflect a return to a preverbal state where feeling precedes thought – what Didier Anzieu (1989) might describe as the "skin ego," a psychic structure grounded in tactile and sensory experiences.

From a relational psychoanalytic lens, Connie's differentiation between solitary and partnered masturbation is equally important. In solitude, she accesses a dissociated self-state – raw, uncensored, non-performative. With Dave, the same act becomes relational, mirrored, and reciprocal, supporting Jessica Benjamin's (2004) theory that sexuality operates across both intrapsychic and intersubjective registers. Connie is not simply comparing two behaviors – she is narrating two psychic positions: one where she reclaims private selfhood, and another where she plays with mutual arousal in the gaze of the other.

Trauma, Memory, and the Language of the Body

Trauma is rarely remembered as a coherent narrative. More often, it lingers in the body as fragments – sensations, impulses, and states that defy language. For survivors of early relational trauma, like Connie, the body may become the first and only container for experiences that were never witnessed, mirrored, or metabolized. Her solitary sexual rituals did not emerge from conscious fantasy or relational play. They were acts of embodied knowing – a private grammar of sound, movement, and intensity that preceded narrative awareness.

What Connie described as "animal-like" or "primal" was not regressive, but restorative. These states weren't performative or theatrical; they were raw expressions of feeling that had never been permitted or seen. Her body was not breaking down – it was speaking in the only language it had access to at the time of the original violation: sensation, rhythm, voice.

Psychoanalyst Dori Laub (1992) reminds us that trauma involves not only the rupture of experience but also the absence of a witness. Connie's body had long carried truths that remained unspoken – not because she lacked words, but because there had never been a space safe enough to receive them. Through her years of therapeutic work, and more recently through her growing curiosity about her masturbation practice, these somatic truths began to emerge – not as flashbacks, but as *felt testimonies*. Each contraction, grunt, and tremor was not merely a discharge of energy. It was a kind of storytelling that she told in breath and muscle, in instinct and release.

From a neurobiological perspective, Connie's experience echoes what Bessel van der Kolk (2014) and others describe as implicit memory: the way trauma is stored not in words but in procedural patterns and autonomic responses. Her post-orgasmic floods of tears weren't incidental – they were her nervous system's delayed effort to metabolize what had once over-whelmed her capacity to feel. This somatic emergence aligns with what Janina Fisher (2021) and Pat Ogden et al. (2006) emphasize: the body tells the story that the mind has not yet formed.

But it wasn't just the act of masturbation that was reparative – it was Connie's attention to it. The noticing. The meaning-making. The willing-ness to share the details, however raw or strange they felt, and to allow them to be witnessed without shame.

This shift – from private ritual to shared exploration – reflects the psy-choanalytic process of *working through* (Freud, 1914): the slow, layered transformation of affect and repetition into integration. Rather than ana-lyzing the orgasm itself, we stayed with what emerged in its wake – grief, relief, the surprise of tenderness. This wasn't a reenactment of trauma. She was moving through it, letting her body grieve what it could not grieve at the time.

Her story also illustrates a paradox at the heart of trauma and sexual-ity: that the very site of violation can, under the right conditions, become a site of restoration. As Holly Richmond (2021) argues, pleasure – when consciously reclaimed – can be a political act, a declaration of sovereignty over the body. Connie wasn't seeking to escape her past. She was seeking to feel it differently. To reclaim what had once been taken from her: her capacity to feel fully and to stay present.

In this way, her solitary orgasm became a kind of somatic symboliza-tion – a nonverbal act that carried unconscious meaning before it could be put into words. As Donald Winnicott (1971a) might suggest, it func-tioned as a transitional phenomenon: a space where she could oscillate between isolation and connection, protection and vulnerability, enactment and emergence. In this private erotic space, she became both subject and object, giver and receiver, child and adult. Her body, long estranged, was becoming known again.

And now, as her therapeutic process neared its natural close, she was finally listening.

Integration and Completion

After several months of openly exploring her masturbation process in ther-apy, Connie expressed that she had arrived at a sense of internal resolution. It wasn't a triumphant breakthrough or a dramatic catharsis. Instead, it was a quiet shift – an embodied knowing that the charge around the ritual had changed. What once felt private, unnameable, and emotionally tangled had become something she could speak about, feel through, and let settle.

Together, we came to understand her solitary sexual practice as a form of *deep somatic release* – a living trace of childhood pain, anger, and shame that had found a private exit route through rhythm, sensation, and breath. Her experience didn't surface in the conventional form of trauma narrative. There were no flashbacks or linear memories. Instead, it emerged through what Dori Laub might call the "missing witness" of the body – a rhythmic, ritualized process where her system could express what had once been unspeakable.

In Somatic Experiencing terms, her process echoed what Peter Levine (1997) describes as completing the defensive cycle – allowing the body to perform the actions it was once prevented from carrying out. Connie wasn't reenacting her trauma, nor was she bypassing it. She was giving her nervous system the chance to move toward completion on its own terms – through contraction and release, intensity and collapse, grief and rest.

From a psychoanalytic perspective, we might think of this as a moment of symbolic contact – where something formerly private, even primitive, could be held in language and relationship. Her masturbation ritual, once shrouded in secrecy and shaped by early experiences, became available for reflection – not to be pathologized or fixed, but to be understood. The act itself didn't change, but her relationship to it did. She could stay with her body, follow its rhythms, and let its truth be known – not just to herself, but within the shared space of therapy.

This is the kind of integration that sometimes unfolds in trauma-informed sex therapy – not a dramatic breakthrough, but a shift in felt meaning. Not a resolution of trauma, but a reweaving of self and sensation. What was once dissociated or exiled could now be spoken, witnessed, and made part of the whole.

Summary of Key Concepts

- **Masturbation can serve as a site of trauma integration,** particularly when it is somatically intense, affectively charged, or ritualistic in nature. Rather than viewing such practices as merely compensatory or symptomatic, therapists can explore their symbolic and reparative functions.
- **Somatic reprocessing** occurs when the body re-engages with frozen trauma through movement, sensation, and affective discharge. Connie's masturbation practice embodied what somatic theorists call "completing the defensive cycle" (Levine, 1997).
- **Solitary sexual practices may access dissociated self-states** – parts of the self that are not yet available to conscious awareness or relational engagement. These states often express themselves in nonverbal, rhythmic, or affectively intense forms.
- **Trauma is stored in implicit memory systems** and often re-emerges through the body, not through conscious recall. Erotic rituals that seem

repetitive or private may carry deep historical meanings tied to attachment, violation, or survival.

- **Therapeutic presence and erotic witnessing** allow for meaning-making. When clients share private erotic material, especially practices that feel "strange" or shameful, it is crucial that clinicians hold these disclosures with safety, warmth, and thoughtful containment.
- **Psychoanalytic and somatic frameworks intersect** meaningfully in trauma-informed sex therapy. Concepts like symbolic enactment, working-through, bodily testimony, and mutual recognition provide clinicians with tools to navigate the complexity of post-traumatic erotic life.
- **Pleasure is not always simple or joyful.** It can be layered with grief, protest, and release. Allowing clients to explore these layered affective states without shame supports deeper healing and reintegration of the erotic self.

For Clinical Reflection

- How do I receive a client's account of solitary sexual practices – what feelings, assumptions, or judgments arise in me?
- Do I make room for nonverbal material – movement, sound, breath – as valid and meaningful clinical data?
- Am I attuned to how a client's masturbation ritual might hold both trauma and transformation?
- Do I rush to interpret, reassure, or normalize sexual behaviors that make me uncomfortable – or can I stay curious?
- What is my own countertransference when a client describes orgasm accompanied by tears, grief, or rage?
- How do I hold the paradox of pleasure that is tangled with pain?
- Am I privileging verbal narrative over embodied experience in my clinical work?
- What internal resources or support do I need to more confidently integrate somatic exploration into psychoanalytic therapy?

Chapter 6

Is Porn to Blame? Rethinking Pornography in Sex Therapy

Pornography in Sex Therapy

Pornography remains one of the most polarizing and misunderstood topics in the field of sexual health. For some clinicians, it is a powerful tool – one that can support fantasy exploration, enhance arousal, and stimulate conversation between partners. For others, it's viewed with deep skepticism, often associated with relational detachment, compulsive use, or sexual dissatisfaction.

In truth, pornography is neither inherently good nor bad – it is a culturally mediated erotic stimulus, and its meaning is always contextual. In my clinical practice, I've seen pornography serve as a catalyst for sexual growth, intimacy, and self-discovery. I've also seen it become a screen – used to avoid vulnerability, mask anxiety, or maintain a sense of control in the face of deeper emotional conflicts.

What matters is not the porn itself, but the function it serves in a person's psychic and relational life. This view aligns with the work of Marty Klein (2010), who argues that clinical discussions of pornography must move beyond moral panic and instead assess how porn functions within the client's erotic and relational landscape. Pornography can be a symptom of something unspoken, or it can be a solution to something unmanageable. Often, it is both.

This chapter explores how pornography use can become entangled with intrapsychic struggle, performance anxiety, and relational disconnection – and how therapy can help unravel those knots. Through the case of Maurice, I demonstrate an integrative therapeutic approach that includes:

- Behavioral interventions to create structure and reduce compulsivity
- Sex script analysis to assess patterns of arousal, initiation, and meaning
- Psychoanalytic exploration of fantasy and unconscious conflict
- Coaching-style experimentation to co-create new sexual scripts with a partner

DOI: 10.4324/9781003318187-7

These layered methods reflect the ethos of this book: that sexual symptoms are often doorways into deeper terrain. When approached with curiosity and care, pornography use can reveal unmet emotional needs, unresolved tension between desire and attachment, and the protective function of fantasy in the face of shame, insecurity, or fear.

The Initial Concern: When the Presenting Problem Isn't the Real Problem

Maurice entered therapy concerned about his drinking. He was a chef at a high-end restaurant and worked late hours. It was customary that the kitchen and wait staff would end the night by going to a bar to unwind and talk about the night. This resulted in him getting home in the early hours of morning, often to have his girlfriend waiting up and angry about the late night drunkenness. They would fight for a few hours before she went to work, and then Maurice would collapse into bed to sleep off the alcohol and the anger. He was exhausted by this cycle and ready to make some changes to his lifestyle.

We talked it over for a few weeks, and he quite easily came up with modifications he wanted to make. He decided that he would allow himself one night per week where he went out with his coworkers after work. The other nights, he would come directly home without having any alcohol. His girlfriend Sasha was happy and in agreement with this schedule, and within a few months, their relationship was in a much better place. Maurice was feeling more confident with himself, both mentally and physically.

Then during a following session, Maurice admitted that it wasn't really his drinking that was causing him the most concern. "I'm glad that I've cut back on my drinking and that I'm fighting less with Sasha. But in all honesty, there is something else that has been more concerning to me."

I find this often to be the case in therapy, and particularly in sex therapy. What someone comes into therapy for is often not the most significant problem. It takes time to build enough safety to disclose what's most vulnerable – especially when it involves sexuality. Concerns about arousal, performance, desire, or porn use often remain unspoken until there is enough trust to tolerate the shame or confusion that may accompany them.

In Maurice's case, the drinking had functioned as a socially acceptable distress signal – a visible symptom that masked more private concerns. This layering of problems – what psychoanalysis refers to as a displacement or a substitute formation – is common in clinical work. Clients often lead with the issue that feels easier to name, while the deeper, more emotionally charged material waits in the wings.

Maurice's shift in focus marked a turning point in our work. It opened the door to understanding not just what he did – drinking, fighting, withdrawing – but why. What was underneath the surface behavior? What anxiety was being managed, what feelings were being bypassed, and how might sexuality be functioning as both a defense and a longing?

Underlying Concerns: Pornography and Erectile Difficulty

"It's not exactly easy to talk about, but here it goes," Maurice said. "Since I spend so much time at home during the day because of my work hours, I tend to watch a lot of porn and masturbate in the afternoons – and I'm worried that maybe it's having a negative effect on my sex drive with Sasha. I've noticed that lately it has been harder for me to stay hard during sex. I'm sure Sasha has noticed too, but she hasn't said anything. And now I'm stuck in my head about it, so I've been avoiding initiating sex. But that doesn't seem to be a great solution either. I don't know what to do at this point."

This kind of disclosure is not uncommon in sex therapy. As with many sexual concerns, Maurice wasn't entirely sure whether his behavior constituted a "problem," but he knew it didn't feel right. He was anxious and preoccupied, uncertain how to distinguish between normal variation in sexual desire and a deeper issue.

There is a fair amount of disagreement in the mental health and sex therapy fields around pornography. Advocates argue that it can be a useful tool for couples to add excitement into their sex lives. It can be a way to engage in fantasy, build arousal, and expand curiosity into an endless variety of sexual practices. For individuals, pornography can support masturbation, allow for the exploration of fetishes and taboos, and even reduce shame by normalizing certain sexual interests.

Critics, however, argue that frequent pornography use can lead to arousal dependency, diminished sensitivity to partnered stimuli, or emotional distancing. The relational aspects of sex – desire negotiation, vulnerability, spontaneity – can feel overwhelming compared to the on-demand, consequence-free stimulation that pornography provides. As a result, clients may begin to rely on porn as a way of bypassing the anxiety, awkwardness, or interpersonal complexity that often accompanies partnered sex.

Maurice's situation exemplified this dynamic. In many ways, pornography had been serving a regulatory function – managing his arousal, soothing his insecurities, and providing a private, controlled erotic space free from the expectations of reciprocity. From a psychoanalytic standpoint, we might say that porn had become a transitional object of sorts: a space in which desire could be felt safely, without the risk of emotional exposure. But as often happens, what initially served a protective function began to limit his erotic flexibility and his relational presence.

Rather than rush to label his behavior as "compulsive" or pathologize his use of porn, I became curious about how the behavior fit into the larger pattern of his life and sexuality. What was the internal logic of Maurice's arousal? What was he avoiding? What was he defending against? And what longings – perhaps unconscious – were embedded in his private erotic ritual?

Assessment: Understanding the Sexual Pattern

As with any sexual issue that comes up in therapy, I began by asking Maurice to describe in as much detail as possible his understanding of the problem. I wanted to explore not just the frequency of his pornography use, but its texture, timing, and meaning. How often did he masturbate to porn, and for how long? Was orgasm always the goal, or was arousal itself part of the reward? What kind of porn did he seek out, and had his preferences changed over time? Was this a recent pattern, or did it have roots earlier in his sexual history?

These questions serve multiple purposes. They help normalize the conversation about sex while also signaling to the client that erotic behavior deserves the same thoughtful inquiry as any other psychological concern. This kind of detailed sexual assessment – central to both psychodynamic and contemporary sex therapy practice – offers a pathway to understanding the function of a behavior, rather than just its frequency or appearance. As Esther Perel often notes, erotic life is rarely about the act itself – it's about the emotional and psychological ecosystem in which it lives.

Maurice described relaxed afternoons of watching pornography for several hours. His typical pattern was to masturbate to orgasm within the first 30 minutes, then continue watching porn throughout the afternoon. Sometimes he would build arousal again before Sasha came home from work, hoping it would carry over into sex.

"It started about a year ago when I noticed not being as turned on during sex with Sasha," Maurice reflected. "It wasn't anything that she was or wasn't doing in bed. I guess it was just that sex was starting to feel routine and a little predictable. Because I work in the evenings, we would have sex when Sasha came home from work and before I left for the evening. I started watching porn to help get me in the mood and turned on before she came home. And it worked for quite a while. I would watch something that turned me on and then use it to fantasize about during sex with Sasha. The problem is that now I have found so much pornography that really turns me on, it is getting more difficult for me to even look forward to sex with Sasha."

Maurice was describing a shift that many clients experience: a gradual recalibration of arousal. What once served as a warm-up now became a necessity – and eventually, a replacement. From a sex therapy standpoint, this progression can signal arousal conditioning – a pattern in which stimulation becomes linked to a very specific context or cue (in this case, porn) and becomes harder to access in different settings (such as partnered sex).

Here, contemporary sex therapy practices – particularly those informed by the dual control model of sexual arousal (Bancroft & Janssen, 2000) – can offer helpful framing. Maurice's arousal system was likely experiencing heightened excitatory response to novelty and visual stimulation, while simultaneously registering higher inhibitory response during real-life sexual encounters that involved emotional pressure, performance anxiety, or relational vulnerability.

But from a psychoanalytic perspective, there was also something deeper at play. Maurice's porn use had become a private space of control, fantasy, and retreat. It wasn't just about sex – it was about soothing, staging, and protecting. In this context, we weren't just talking about erectile function – we were talking about the unconscious choreography of desire.

Fantasy Content: Exploring the Significance of Preferred Material

"Can you tell me about the pornography that you are watching? Is there something in particular that you find yourself being drawn to?" I asked.

Maurice responded, "At first it was just the novelty of looking at pornography that was fun. It didn't really matter much. But now I have become obsessed with watching porn where there is an older woman who seduces a younger man. There is something about the fantasy of being pursued that is a big turn on. And I can find endless varieties of this scenario and get lost in a rabbit hole of porn."

Maurice and I spent a considerable amount of time talking about this fantasy and the different scenarios that appealed to him, but somehow we didn't seem to be getting much traction in understanding the issue at hand. Then it dawned on me: I was getting as distracted with the pornography as Maurice was – trying to figure out what it was about being pursued that was so appealing to him. I found myself captivated by the specificity of the scenes, the recurring themes of seduction and surrender, and the emotional charge that seemed to animate them.

This is when the psychoanalytic frame became both a tool and a challenge. Exploring, reflecting, and interpreting unconscious dynamics is central to our work, but when it comes to sex, we must be careful not to get lost in meaning at the expense of embodiment. It's one of the classic tensions between traditional psychoanalysis and contemporary sex therapy: the risk of over-symbolizing erotic material without attending to the body's role in desire and arousal.

Maurice's fantasies were rich with psychological significance, but they were also part of a lived sexual experience – one that included visual arousal, masturbation, and physical release. In sex therapy, we are trained to explore both: the meaning and the mechanics. We want to know the specific details of how a sexual experience unfolds – the sex script – because arousal doesn't exist in the abstract. It exists in rhythm, pacing, body position, sensory input, emotional tone. It's in these nuances that we often find the answers to why something feels arousing – or why something suddenly doesn't.

Maurice's fantasy of being pursued by an older woman carried an unmistakable psychological logic. It offered a reversal of his current relational dynamics: he was no longer the one initiating or caretaking, no longer responsible for setting the tone or maintaining the emotional atmosphere. In these fantasies, he was wanted – unquestionably, unapologetically – and that wanting had a gravitational pull. He didn't have to perform, he didn't have to lead, he didn't have to guess what was expected of him. He could surrender.

This led us into deeper questions: What emotional function was this fantasy serving? What was it protecting against? What deeper longing might be hidden within the excitement?

Rather than rush to interpret the fantasy, I stayed close to its emotional tone. Staying with the fantasy, rather than dissecting it prematurely, helped Maurice feel seen in his desire rather than pathologized by it. What was the quality of arousal? Was it tied to power? To freedom? To escape? What was the role of agency – and what was the role of helplessness?

As Suzanne Iasenza (2020b) emphasizes, sexual fantasies are not merely symptoms to decode but experiences that can affirm agency, foster arousal, and support the client's evolving sexual self.

Fantasy, from a psychoanalytic perspective, is often both wish and defense. It reveals desire but also protects against anxiety. In Maurice's case, the excitement of being seduced seemed to hold something more – a longing to be chosen, perhaps, or to be relieved of some unspoken weight. At this point in our work, we didn't yet know exactly what that weight was. But we were beginning to trace its outline.

As Michael Bader (2002) explains, sexual fantasies often serve a dual purpose – they are both revealing and protective. They allow people to experience powerful emotional states, such as desire or surrender, in a context that minimizes psychological risk. In Maurice's case, the fantasy gave him access to a version of himself that felt deeply wanted – without the burden of performance or the fear of rejection. It softened the edges of relational pressure and created an internal space where he could safely play out dynamics that felt too vulnerable to express directly.

Rather than treating the fantasy as a barrier to "real sex," we began to view it as a portal into Maurice's erotic intelligence – an adaptive expression of both his needs and his defenses. What emerged wasn't pathology, but a creative solution to an emotional dilemma he hadn't yet been able to name aloud.

Sex Script Analysis: Examining the Details of Sexual Interaction

In his book *So Tell Me About the Last Time You Had Sex*, author and sex therapist Ian Kerner talks extensively about analyzing the sex script for clues of where emotional or erotic connection may falter. The sex script is more than a sequence of behaviors – it's a living narrative where unconscious expectations, embodied habits, relational patterns, and emotional longings unfold. As Kerner writes, "The sexual script is where everything unfolds – the psychology, the emotions, the communication, and the pleasure. It's where couples either connect or disconnect." In Maurice's case, it was within the details of his sexual routine with Sasha that his anxiety, arousal difficulties, and unmet needs were hiding in plain sight.

I asked Maurice to tell me about the last time he and Sasha had sex. He let out a sigh and shook his head. "It's just bad. I don't know where to start."

Recognizing that bad sex can be difficult and humiliating to talk about, I took the lead. In sex therapy, it is essential that we become comfortable talking directly about sex and asking specific questions. This is not the time to wait for the client to initiate. Sexual shame often breeds silence, and therapeutic passivity can unintentionally reinforce the client's sense that something is too embarrassing or unacceptable to name.

"Okay," I said gently, "let's try and really break this down."

I asked Maurice a series of questions about how sex typically got initiated between him and Sasha, what the progression of a typical encounter looked like, and what he noticed about his arousal, emotion, and bodily response throughout. What I learned was that Maurice was the one who always initiated sex and that they had settled into a fairly predictable routine.

Maurice would start by giving Sasha a massage – her shoulders, feet, or back – helping her unwind from the day. Sasha appreciated this and was always receptive. He would then begin to kiss her neck and shoulders, gradually helping her undress. Once she was naked, he would continue with soft kisses before performing oral sex on her, which often led to her orgasm. At this point, I paused to reflect to Maurice that he seemed like an attentive and generous lover, someone deeply attuned to Sasha's pleasure.

"Yes," he acknowledged. "But this is where the problem starts. In the past, I would have an erection the entire time. It really turned me on to watch Sasha relax and unwind. She would let out these deep sighs of pleasure that were so sexy to me – it was like she was turning her body over to me and opening herself up to feeling good."

He paused, then added, "After she had her orgasm, she would usually go down on me for a little while, and then we'd have intercourse until I finished. But now I'm not hard, and it's so embarrassing when she goes to give me head and I'm soft. Watching porn helped give me something to fantasize about that would usually keep me hard, but it doesn't always work anymore. Usually I just blame it on being distracted by work, but I can't keep using that excuse. Now it's just easier to avoid having sex altogether. And because I'm masturbating so much during the day, it doesn't bother me at all to go without."

This kind of avoidance isn't uncommon. When a sexual pattern becomes a source of anxiety or shame, many clients instinctively pull back – not necessarily from desire, but from the vulnerability of revealing their difficulty. From a contemporary sex therapy standpoint, this is where de-shaming the process becomes critical. We must separate performance from self-worth, and sexual difficulty from failure. Maurice was carrying the burden of arousal as a measure of masculinity and love, a weight that had grown heavier as the routine became more scripted and less erotically alive.

From a psychoanalytic perspective, the predictability of the sex script had also taken on a defensive quality. In its repetition, it offered safety – but also rigidity. There was little room for spontaneity, desire, or mutual play. The pleasure was one-directional: focused on Sasha's enjoyment, with Maurice performing the role of caretaker. His arousal depended on her pleasure, and when that wasn't enough to sustain an erection, he was left with a deepening sense of failure and disconnection.

This is often the paradox of well-intentioned sexual caretaking: when one partner consistently assumes the role of provider, it can flatten the erotic field and obscure their own needs, fantasies, and frustrations. In Maurice's case, his attentiveness was genuine, but it was also masking something else – something that would begin to emerge more fully in the conversations to follow.

Therapeutic Reframing: Contextualizing Sexual Difficulties

It's at this point in the discussion – after gathering a clear sense of the sexual pattern and script – that I often offer clients a broader framework for understanding what's happening, both sexually and emotionally. Widening the lens in this way invites clients to step out of the binary of "dysfunction" or "failure" and into a more compassionate, contextualized view of their erotic life.

Maurice had described two distinct but intertwined realities: on one hand, extended afternoons of solitary pornography use and masturbation, often involving highly stimulating fantasy scenarios; on the other hand, a steady decline in sexual interest and performance during his intimate encounters with Sasha. He was becoming increasingly disconnected from his own body during partnered sex, and increasingly reliant on porn to stay aroused.

I summarized: "So on the one hand, you're spending a lot of time masturbating to porn – especially scenes where a younger man is seduced by an older woman. That helped you stay aroused for a while, but it's not really working anymore. And on the other hand, sex with Sasha has started to feel predictable, and you're noticing difficulties with getting or staying hard. That's understandably leading to avoidance, which gives you some relief in the short term – but it's also reinforcing the very disconnection you're trying to resolve."

Maurice nodded slowly. "Yeah," he said. "That's the depressing story. And the drinking was a good escape from it all, but I see how that was just causing more problems with Sasha. I just don't know what to do about this part."

This was a pivotal moment in the therapy – not just because Maurice was open to reframing the issue, but because he was beginning to link his sexual concerns to a broader emotional context. Rather than locating the problem solely in his body or behavior, we were beginning to map it across domains of anxiety, relational dynamic, and self-perception.

In contemporary sex therapy, especially when integrating psychoanalytic and behavioral frames, reframing serves as both intervention and alliance-building. It affirms the client's distress while loosening the grip of shame. It invites curiosity instead of diagnosis. And it provides the foundation from which new erotic scripts can emerge – not by fixing the client, but by understanding the ecosystem in which the "problem" has developed.

Behavioral Intervention: Structure and Boundaries

Maurice was an action-oriented person. He liked to feel in motion, to solve problems, and to know he was being productive. That's often a strength in therapy – especially when paired with insight – but it can also reflect an underlying anxiety about sitting with discomfort. For Maurice, the avoidance of sex had become a way to regulate the anxiety he felt around his own sexual performance. Now, with his defenses slightly lowered and the shame named but held, he was open to taking practical steps.

I took a behavioral approach with him, drawing on what had already worked in our early sessions. "Would you want to take the same approach with this as you did with the drinking?" I asked. "What would it be like to put some structure around your pornography and masturbation use? Could you imagine reducing the frequency a bit – not as a punishment, but as an experiment? What would feel manageable?"

Framing the intervention as a collaborative experiment is central to contemporary sex therapy. This approach helps shift clients out of all-or-nothing thinking, and invites them into a more mindful, observational stance toward their own sexual behavior. Rather than moralize or restrict, we co-create parameters that allow for exploration, flexibility, and feedback.

Maurice decided to give himself one day per week to masturbate to porn. It felt like a reasonable experiment – something concrete he could try without feeling deprived or exposed. Within the first two weeks, he noticed an immediate shift. He felt more sexually energized and less numbed out. The overstimulation and compulsive edge of his daily porn use had softened, and his baseline desire for Sasha began to return.

But what also emerged, perhaps even more importantly, was a wave of performance anxiety. Without the cushion of porn and solo pleasure earlier in the day, Maurice was more acutely aware of the pressure he felt during sex. He worried about whether he would be able to get hard, whether Sasha would notice, and what it would mean about him if he didn't. His reduced porn use had helped his physical responsiveness, but it had also exposed the underlying emotional strain he was carrying into sexual encounters.

This is often the case when behavioral change happens ahead of emotional processing. What initially appears to be improvement – more desire, more arousal – can stir up deeper insecurities that were previously masked by habit or avoidance. That doesn't mean the intervention failed. It means the real work is now possible.

Maurice was beginning to see the relationship between his daily porn ritual and his internal regulation system. Porn had helped him manage uncertainty, predict stimulation, and avoid disappointment. Now, with that buffer reduced, he was left to face the relational stakes of sex – and the pressure he placed on himself to perform, to satisfy, and to prove his worth.

Psychoanalytic Exploration: Fantasy as a Window to Deeper Issues

Introducing more context to the situation, I asked Maurice if he saw any parallels between the fantasy of being seduced and the sex script he had described with Sasha. Rather than offering a direct interpretation, I floated the idea as a possibility to consider. I was curious whether the fantasy of being pursued might offer him a break from the pressure to initiate, to perform, or to ensure his partner's satisfaction. In all of his fantasies, the older woman was the one taking the lead – hungry, assertive, and in control. Maurice, by contrast, was the object of desire, the recipient of her attention. His arousal was not rooted in dominance or action, but in surrender.

"I hadn't really thought about it that way," he said. "But it makes sense. I do feel a lot of pressure to make sure that Sasha feels loved and sexually satisfied. She works so hard at her career, and the truth is that it's her income that mostly supports our lifestyle. I want to make sure I can bring equal worth to the relationship through love and sex."

He paused. "I've actually been wanting to propose to her. But I'm nervous. I worry she might not be as committed as I am – especially after the drinking issue, and now this sex stuff."

This moment marked a crucial deepening in our work. Maurice's fantasy, while overtly sexual, had always been about more than just arousal. It was about emotional reversal. In his day-to-day life, he felt responsible, subordinate, and unsure of his place in the relationship. The fantasy offered an alternate reality: one in which he was irresistible, desired, and relieved of pressure. He didn't have to pursue or impress – he only had to receive.

In psychoanalytic terms, this fantasy provided a protective function. It created a space where dependency and desire could coexist without humiliation. In real life, the vulnerability of wanting – especially in the context of financial inequality, past conflict, and relational insecurity – felt too dangerous to fully express. But in the fantasy, Maurice could be overtaken by someone else's desire. There was no risk of rejection or judgment. Only pleasure, inevitability, and surrender.

This kind of erotic reversal is not uncommon in fantasy life. Sexual fantasies often function as symbolic resolutions to real-life conflicts – offering agency where there is helplessness, control where there is chaos, and acceptance where there is anxiety. Jean Laplanche's theory of sexuality as shaped by enigmatic messages from early caregivers offers one lens here: we are drawn not just to what arouses us, but to what helps us metabolize unformulated emotional experience. In Maurice's case, the fantasy wasn't just erotic – it was stabilizing. It gave shape to an otherwise disorganizing inner state.

This understanding was also supported by contemporary sex research. Justin Lehmiller's work on fantasy reveals that most people's sexual fantasies are psychologically rich, not merely sexually novel. They often offer insight into unmet needs – affection, control, nurturance, validation. Maurice's growing awareness of the emotional charge embedded in his fantasy allowed us to start treating it not as a problem to fix, but as a portal into something more real, more relational, and more open to change.

As we explored further, Maurice began to link his seduction fantasy with the larger pressures he was feeling in his life. Financial stress, career insecurity, and relational ambiguity had all converged to create a sense of helplessness. The fantasy allowed him to reclaim a sense of potency – not through power, but through being wanted. In this way, fantasy became not just a place of escape, but a mirror – reflecting his internal struggle and pointing toward his longing for reassurance, freedom, and desire that felt unconditional.

Multidimensional Approach: Addressing Life Issues Beyond Sexuality

Staying consistent with the proactive tone of our work, Maurice and I began to explore the broader context of his life. The deeper we went into the emotional underpinnings of his fantasy, the clearer it became that his sexual concerns weren't isolated – they were threaded through with his sense of agency, identity, and worth. This is often the case in therapy. Sexual symptoms don't exist in a vacuum; they're shaped and sustained by the wider landscape of a client's relational, professional, and intrapsychic world.

We started with the area that felt most tangible: work. Maurice had been feeling undervalued in his job for quite some time, and we devised a plan and timeline for him to ask for a raise. He rehearsed the conversation in session, anticipating possible outcomes. He returned the following week and proudly shared that he had successfully negotiated a raise. This boost in income and confidence had a ripple effect: it restored a sense of adult competence that had previously felt compromised, especially in the context of Sasha's higher earning power.

At the same time, we opened up space for him to talk more honestly with Sasha about their relationship and future. He shared his hesitancy around proposing, his fear of rejection, and his desire for more clarity around her level of commitment. To his relief, Sasha had also been thinking about marriage, and the conversation opened a pathway for more direct communication. They came up with a shared timeline for engagement, which gave Maurice a newfound sense of security and motivation.

This multidimensional shift – addressing the practical, relational, and emotional aspects of his life – marked a turning point. With his self-esteem no longer tethered solely to his sexual performance or role in the relationship, Maurice found that his preoccupation with porn and masturbation began to ease. It wasn't that he lost interest in solo pleasure; rather, it no longer functioned as his primary coping strategy.

In contemporary sex therapy, it's crucial to treat sexual issues within the full context of the client's life. Focusing solely on the symptom can lead to short-term change without long-term transformation. By linking Maurice's erotic anxiety to his financial insecurity, relational uncertainty, and sense of agency, we were able to shift the work from symptom management to identity development.

From a psychoanalytic perspective, we might say that Maurice was beginning to strengthen his ego function – not in a defensive way, but in a way that allowed him to hold multiple truths at once: that he could feel unsure and still act; that he could want reassurance and still show initiative; that he could fantasize about surrender while practicing leadership in his own life. His growth wasn't just about becoming more aroused – it was about becoming more integrated.

Sexual Coaching: Introducing New Erotic Scripts

With this newfound emotional momentum – more confidence at work, a clearer sense of relational security – Maurice began to feel more grounded in himself. This stability opened the door for erotic curiosity. He described feeling more sexually confident and noted a shift in his fantasies: "I've been having these slightly dominant thoughts . . . like tying Sasha up with a silk scarf while I touch her."

This was a meaningful development. Maurice was moving from a fantasy of being pursued and passively desired into one where he initiated sensation, structured the scene, and played with power. The tone was not aggressive or controlling; it was imaginative and playful. He was beginning to explore a more expressive erotic self – one that could act on desire, not just react to it.

I encouraged him to share the fantasy with Sasha and see how she responded. She found it exciting and suggested they try it. Together in session, Maurice and I imagined how he might set the scene: using a soft scarf, playing with different sensations like ice, feathers, or gentle biting. These elements weren't just "spicing things up" – they were shifting the erotic script. We were working not only with fantasy content, but with the structure of arousal itself.

One key piece of this work was helping Maurice decouple erection from sexual success. I encouraged him to avoid ending the experience with intercourse. The goal was to reduce pressure on penetrative sex and allow for new, embodied experiences of pleasure and connection. This also interrupted the habitual script in which his anxiety about erection dictated the tempo of the encounter. Instead of monitoring his body, Maurice could focus on the scene, the sensations, and Sasha's response.

Maurice later reported that the experience was a success – not because everything "worked perfectly," but because the dynamic had changed. Sasha found it thrilling to be lightly restrained, which seemed to intensify her sensations and focus. Maurice, in turn, felt turned on by her responsiveness and by allowing himself to take up more erotic space. Because he wasn't preoccupied with whether or not he had an erection, he felt more present. He noticed that at times he was hard, and at times he wasn't – and that Sasha didn't seem to mind either way.

In contemporary sex therapy, especially within a coaching framework, sensate creativity is key. New erotic scripts don't have to be elaborate or extreme – they just need to interrupt old patterns and offer enough novelty to reignite interest and connection. What we're aiming for isn't perfect sex – it's expanded sexual possibility.

This experience showed Maurice that he wasn't trapped by his previous sexual pattern. He could re-enter erotic connection on new terms – less pressured, more playful, more connected to both himself and his partner.

Integration and Growth: Redefining the Sexual Relationship

Through our ongoing conversations and embodied experimentation, Maurice began to feel more comfortable talking about sex and sharing his fantasies with Sasha. What started as a highly private and shame-tinged internal world gradually became something relational – something he could co-create with his partner.

As the therapy progressed, our work shifted further into a collaborative, coaching-based model. Maurice began introducing a wider range of fantasies into their sexual life, including the "older woman seduces younger man" scenario that had initially felt too embarrassing to name aloud. To his relief, Sasha didn't reject it – in fact, she enjoyed the vitality and playfulness that their shared fantasy exploration brought to their intimacy. She was happy to engage in role-playing, which made Maurice feel more accepted and seen.

They created a recurring scene where Sasha would "catch" Maurice watching pornography when she came home from work. After a playful scolding, she would step into the role of the older, dominant woman and take charge of the sexual encounter – usually leading to Maurice receiving oral sex as the culmination of the scene. There was a touch of humor, a healthy dose of erotic tension, and most importantly, a new sense of mutual engagement.

They even began scheduling a weekly "sex date" to anchor these experiences. It became something they both looked forward to, a time set aside not just for physical connection but for creative collaboration. During the week, they would discuss variations on their fantasies – ways to keep the scenes fresh, responsive, and exciting. Maurice, who had once felt disconnected and anxious in his sexuality, was now imagining, anticipating, and participating with more openness and ease.

At times, they watched pornography together – particularly more realistic, ethically produced content that felt relatable and emotionally resonant. What had once been a private escape for Maurice had become a shared tool for discovery. Pornography wasn't banned or vilified – it was contextualized. It had moved from a symptom of avoidance to a source of shared arousal and erotic inspiration.

This kind of erotic repair doesn't come from eliminating old behaviors, but from reimagining their function. Maurice hadn't "given up" pornography; he had reintegrated it into a relational framework. He hadn't conquered his performance anxiety by mastering erections, but by shifting the meaning of arousal itself. Sexual success was no longer measured in minutes or firmness – it was measured in connection, presence, and play.

From a psychoanalytic perspective, we could say Maurice had worked through a key internal conflict: his fear that being desired required performance. Instead, he discovered that being wanted could be felt and enjoyed – even in moments of vulnerability, even without an erection, even with laughter and improvisation. From a sex therapy standpoint, Maurice had moved from avoidance and inhibition toward a more flexible, resilient erotic self.

Conclusion: Pornography as a Tool Rather Than a Problem

Maurice's case illustrates several essential principles in sex therapy. First, the initial presenting problem – drinking – was not the whole story. It functioned as a protective cover for a more vulnerable and less socially acceptable concern: erectile anxiety and a growing dependence on pornography. This progression is common in therapy, especially when sexual shame makes it difficult to name the real issue at the outset.

Second, sexual concerns rarely exist in isolation. Maurice's arousal difficulties were shaped not only by behavioral habits, but also by unresolved anxiety, career insecurity, and relational uncertainty. His use of pornography wasn't inherently pathological, but it had become fused with avoidance – of performance pressure, of emotional exposure, and of his own unmet needs.

Third, pornography itself is not the problem. Like any erotic stimulus, its meaning depends on context. It can serve as a vehicle for fantasy, a source of stimulation, or a numbing tool to bypass relational discomfort.

The key therapeutic question is never "How much porn is too much?" but rather, "What function is it serving? And is that function helping or hindering this person's capacity for relational and erotic connection?"

Maurice's therapeutic journey moved through several phases: behavioral structure, fantasy exploration, sex script revision, and relational experimentation. He addressed his career stagnation, clarified his relationship intentions, and practiced new erotic roles with Sasha. Along the way, his relationship to pornography changed – not because he eliminated it, but because it was no longer the only place where his erotic imagination could safely live.

This multidimensional process reflects how contemporary sex therapy benefits from an integrative approach: blending behavioral strategies with psychoanalytic inquiry, relational awareness with erotic coaching. Maurice didn't just become more sexually functional – he became more emotionally available, more creatively engaged, and more at ease in his own erotic skin.

In the end, Maurice went from using pornography as a way to manage anxiety and avoid communication, to using it as a playful and mutual enhancement tool within his relationship. Though we didn't focus heavily on his family-of-origin dynamics, we remained true to a psychoanalytic sensibility: looking beneath the symptom, listening for unconscious meaning, and following the thread of fantasy to a deeper self-understanding.

Maurice's story affirms one of the core themes of this book: that sexuality is not merely a behavior to regulate but a window into the unconscious – a place where conflict and creativity coexist, and where growth becomes possible when we dare to look beneath the surface.

Summary of Key Concepts

- **Pornography use is not inherently pathological.** Its clinical significance lies in its function – whether it facilitates connection, supports fantasy exploration, or reinforces avoidance, shame, or emotional detachment.
- **Presenting problems often mask deeper sexual concerns,** particularly when shame or relational anxiety inhibits direct disclosure. In Maurice's case, drinking was a proxy for unspoken distress around erectile function and arousal.
- **Sexual difficulties are rarely isolated issues.** They often reflect broader emotional and relational patterns – such as performance anxiety, financial insecurity, unresolved attachment needs, or a lack of erotic novelty.
- **Sex scripts hold important diagnostic and intervention clues.** Exploring the structure, pacing, and emotional tone of partnered sex can reveal where arousal breaks down and what deeper dynamics are at play.

- **Erotic fantasies offer a window into unconscious longing and protective mechanisms.** Maurice's fantasy of being seduced allowed him to access desire while relieving performance pressure and reclaiming a sense of worthiness.
- **Integrative sex therapy blends behavioral, psychoanalytic, and coaching strategies,** moving from structure and insight to experimentation and growth. Maurice's case illustrates how clients can shift from avoidance to creative engagement with sexuality.
- **Pornography can be transformed from a solitary coping strategy into a shared erotic tool,** when therapists help clients explore its meaning and reintegrate it into partnered sexual connection.

For Clinical Reflection

- When a client presents with a nonsexual concern like substance use, do I remain curious about whether a sexual concern is quietly waiting underneath?
- How do I assess the function of pornography use in a client's life – emotionally, relationally, and erotically – before jumping to assumptions about frequency or impact?
- Am I comfortable initiating detailed questions about sexual scripts, including initiation, pacing, arousal, and emotional dynamics?
- When a client shares a fantasy that feels charged or embarrassing, can I stay with the fantasy as a source of insight, without rushing to normalize or interpret?
- What unconscious countertransference might I experience in cases involving pornography, performance anxiety, or shifting power dynamics in sex?
- How can I introduce behavioral interventions like "masturbation structure" or "coached fantasy play" without framing them as fixes – but instead as invitations into mindful experimentation?
- In what ways might I support couples in transforming a source of private distress (such as porn) into a shared site of erotic creativity and relational play?

Chapter 7

Binging on Sex
Transforming Compulsive Sexual Behavior

Theoretical Foundations: Compulsion, Repetition, and Symbolic Meaning

The integration of psychoanalytic theory and sex therapy provides a powerful framework for understanding and treating clients whose sexual behaviors reflect deeper psychological conflicts. When sexual behavior feels compulsive or out of control, it is often not about sex per se, but about regulation – of affect, of unmet needs, and of psychic pain that has never found a home in language or relationship. These behaviors can be viewed as symbolic enactments, rooted in early relational trauma and fueled by unconscious attempts to gain mastery over overwhelming internal states.

The concept of repetition compulsion, first articulated by Freud, offers a foundational lens through which to understand this dynamic. Rather than simply seeking pleasure, individuals may find themselves reenacting painful or traumatic interpersonal scenarios in their sexual lives, driven by the unconscious hope of transforming an early wound. Yet in seeking resolution, they often recreate the very dynamics they seek to escape, reinforcing old injuries rather than healing them.

Contemporary psychoanalytic thinkers have expanded on Freud's formulation. Jessica Benjamin (1990, 2004) describes how trauma can collapse the space for mutual recognition, leaving individuals caught in asymmetrical relationships where they alternate between submission and control. In this light, compulsive sexual behavior may reflect a desperate effort to be seen, to assert agency, or to make contact – albeit in ways that repeat rather than repair developmental injury.

From a trauma-informed lens, clinicians such as Janina Fisher (2021) and Pat Ogden (2006) remind us that trauma often leaves its imprint not just on the mind, but on the body. In these cases, sexual behavior may be an attempt to regulate dysregulated nervous systems, fragmenting self-states, or somatic memories that haven't yet been integrated into conscious experience. Bessel van der Kolk's seminal work (2014) also supports this view,

DOI: 10.4324/9781003318187-8

noting that trauma can disrupt the capacity to feel bodily ownership and pleasure. For some clients, sex becomes either anesthetic or compulsive – a dissociative strategy rather than a relational one.

The Out-of-Control Sexual Behavior (OCSB) model, developed by Braun-Harvey and Vigorito (2016), provides a compelling alternative to the traditional sex addiction framework. Rather than pathologizing desire or labeling individuals as addicts, the OCSB model centers the misalignment between a person's values and behaviors. It focuses on restoring sexual health by helping clients explore what they want from their sexuality – and what's getting in the way. This approach fosters self-compassion and reduces shame while still holding space for accountability and change.

When combined with the behavioral interventions, mindfulness practices, and psychoeducational tools of modern sex therapy, the psychoanalytic model adds depth and symbolic meaning. Together, these approaches allow us to understand compulsive sexual behavior not as a character flaw or moral failing, but as a symptom that speaks. Sexual symptoms are often messages from the unconscious – communications about unmet needs, dissociated feelings, and unresolved conflicts that have not yet found safe relational ground.

In the case that follows, Joelle's cycle of binging on sex, alcohol, and food is explored through this integrated framework. Rather than labeling her behavior as pathological or addictive, the therapy supports her in slowing down the compulsive cycle, becoming curious about her sexual script, and reclaiming her body as a source of pleasure, rather than a battleground for unresolved grief, rage, and shame.

Case Summary

Joelle entered therapy after a weekend of binging on food, alcohol, and sex. On Friday night, she hooked up with a random man that she met at her neighborhood bar. She wasn't attracted to him, but he bought her a few drinks, and she felt obligated to say yes when he asked to walk her home. She knew that he was looking to hook up by the way he was flirting with her. She told herself that she would play it cool and find a way to avoid any physical contact with him. But when he started kissing her, she found it was easier to just go along. She didn't know how to say no. So she did what had become a pattern for her. She told herself to just go for it and invited him upstairs, where she spent the next few hours getting more drunk and having sex that she barely remembered in the morning. She hoped that he would leave that morning without wanting more sex, but that rarely happened. Joelle was an attractive young woman who received a lot of male attention. Again, she decided it would be easier to get the sex over with, so she woke him up by giving him a blow job. When he finally left, she spent the rest of the morning binging on food. But when he called her later that afternoon inviting her to dinner, she said yes. "Who cares," she thought. "At least I'll get a free dinner out of it and it's better than staying home feeling depressed." And so the pattern continued for another two nights. It was a pattern that repeated itself often, with many different men. More drinking, more unwanted sex, and more binging.

This kind of pattern, seen through a psychoanalytic sex therapy lens, is rarely about impulse alone. Rather than viewing Joelle's behavior as purely self-destructive, we can understand it as an unconscious repetition of earlier relational dynamics – scenarios where her agency was compromised, her worth was conditional, and her body became a site of relational exchange. What appears as "binging" on sex may, in fact, be a reenactment of early object relations: receiving something (attention, dinner, approval) in exchange for emotional and bodily surrender. The sex is not about pleasure; it is about survival.

As Joelle described this weekend to me, she oscillated between expressing shame and pride. At times, she broke down crying and seemed broken and defeated. Joelle described a complicated history of binging and purging all through high school and college. At one point early on in college, she felt so out of control with her eating that she became suicidal and was admitted to an inpatient eating disorder treatment program. She was ashamed that she was binging on food again, despite having successfully managed her eating disorder for the past five years. She also recognized that her binging on food only happened after a night of drinking and casual sex.

Joelle described feeling angry at herself for hooking up with men that she wasn't attracted to or interested in. But it was nearly impossible for her to turn down sexual advances. There was a moment of vulnerability as Joelle described this difficulty. She began to softly cry, and said something happened where she just froze in those moments. She didn't want to hurt the person's feelings by rejecting them, and she felt an obligation to give them sex if they had paid for her dinner or drinks.

This description is consistent with what many trauma-informed clinicians recognize as fawn and freeze responses – submissive survival strategies often employed by individuals who learned early that care and danger came from the same source. Joelle's body knew how to comply when she sensed an expectation to please – especially in response to perceived obligation or transactional dynamics – even if it meant disconnecting from her own desire.

She also acknowledged that there was something about "being wanted" that was too hard for her to resist. She then cried deeply, saying that she'd never felt wanted her whole life.

This statement – so simple and so devastating – offered a glimpse into the depth of Joelle's pain, but not yet an opening for change. At this stage of treatment, her sexual behavior still functioned as both a defense and a cry for contact. She could articulate the shame and confusion, but she wasn't yet asking why. From a psychoanalytic sex therapy perspective, this is not unusual. In the early phases of therapy, clients often oscillate between collapse and defiance, between craving intimacy and pushing it away. Joelle's disclosure marked a critical moment of emotional contact, but not yet reflective integration. My task, at this point, was to hold the space – attuning to the symbolic weight of her behavior without rushing to interpret or fix. Change would come later, but for now, we had to stay with the pain.

Developmental History and Family Dynamics

Joelle is an only child whose parents divorced when she was 6 years old. Her father was having an affair and left Joelle's mother to marry the other woman, whom he eventually had two other children with. Growing up, Joelle had regular contact with her father and his new family but always felt like the outsider in their home and that she didn't belong. She also described her father as a withdrawn person in general and said that their interactions always felt somewhat distant and awkward.

From a psychoanalytic perspective, Joelle's experience with her father may be seen as an early narcissistic injury – a foundational sense of not being wanted, mirrored, or emotionally recognized. His detachment likely shaped the internalized belief that she was unworthy of consistent attention or belonging. In this way, the emotional template for later romantic encounters was established: proximity without attunement, presence without protection.

She described her mother, on the other hand, as highly narcissistic and invasive. Joelle recounted that after the divorce, her mother would often speak negatively about her father. She would ask Joelle to tell her specific details about his life with his new family. This put Joelle in a very difficult predicament. If she was honest about feeling out of place at her father's house, her mother would become outraged and it reinforced the narrative that Joelle's father had abandoned them and didn't love them. This would trigger not only her mother's anger, but also her despair. Joelle's mother would become overwhelmed with sadness. Joelle spent many nights consoling her grief-stricken mother.

Here, we see the collapse of the parental function into a form of emotional enmeshment. Joelle was required to regulate her mother's affect, becoming both confidante and emotional caretaker. The child's needs were eclipsed by the parent's pain. This kind of boundary violation, common in children of narcissistically organized parents, often results in what Janina Fisher (2021) describes as a fragmented self-state: one part desperately seeking love and approval, another protecting against annihilation by complying, caretaking, or dissociating.

Joelle's mother also struggled with an undiagnosed eating disorder. She was obsessed over food and was intensely focused on her appearance. Joelle grew up watching her mom count calories and restrict certain foods. There was a lot of discussion about good foods and bad foods. As Joelle became older, she was included in the weekly weigh-ins and the scheduled exercise that her mother lived by. By the time Joelle was an early teen, she was binging and purging in secret. She described binging as a way to sneak and indulge in forbidden foods and purging was a way to keep her weight down and maintain her mother's approval.

In this dynamic, the body becomes both a battleground and a bargaining chip. The compulsive regulation of food mirrored her mother's attempt to impose control in the face of emotional chaos. Joelle's own eating disorder can be seen not only as a defense against overwhelming feelings but also as a mode of identification with her mother's values: beauty, control, perfection, sacrifice. At the same time, it was a rebellion – a secret indulgence, a private refusal. This dialectic of compliance and defiance would later re-emerge in Joelle's sexual behavior.

She described a confusing contradiction of feeling invisible to her mother, while at the same time feeling that her appearance was constantly being scrutinized and controlled.

This paradox – being seen and unseen at once – is central to many trauma-based relational injuries. Joelle's sexual encounters, later in life, carried a haunting echo of this split: craving recognition, but only receiving objectification; fearing invisibility, but finding visibility only through submission. Her erotic symptoms were not meaningless – they were loaded with unconscious material from her early life. Sex had become the stage on which Joelle unconsciously played out the unresolved drama of her childhood: longing, shame, exposure, and abandonment.

Initial Presentation in Therapy

There were two primary ways that Joelle's affect presented itself in session. When talking about her eating disorder and her struggle with binging, Joelle revealed her vulnerability. She described her struggle with anxiety and self-loathing. She cried often in these sessions as she remembered the panic she would feel after a night of binging and the accompanying shame that always followed. She described feeling defeated and hopeless while remembering her mother's inconsolable grief after the divorce. Binging became a way to numb herself and offered a form of control, albeit maladaptive.

From a trauma-informed lens, we can understand Joelle's binging as a form of affective self-regulation – a way to manage internal states that were never safely witnessed, held, or metabolized in early relationships. As in many compulsive behaviors, the binge served as both anesthetic and communication. While Joelle may have felt defeated, her behavior was not just destructive – it was expressive. It was the body trying to speak.

Like all addictions, they initially work to numb painful feelings. Eventually the underlying feelings find a way out. Therapy can interrupt the addictive process by allowing the feelings to be identified, acknowledged, and expressed. One healing aspect of therapy is the witnessing of emotional pain and the opportunity to work through the emotional wounds.

This sentence encapsulates a key principle of both psychoanalytic and trauma-informed treatment: that symptoms are calls for recognition. The therapist's job is not simply to stop the behavior but to help the client begin to name what the behavior is trying to say.

The other way that Joelle's affect presented itself was through anger and defensiveness. When talking about her sexuality, she often led with anger. "Why can't I fuck whoever I want? Why shouldn't I enjoy my sexuality? Why is it okay for men to be admired for their sexual prowess, but not for women? Why should I feel ashamed for having casual sex?" These were all statements that Joelle made when talking about her relationship to her body and her sexuality.

What we witnessed here was a splitting of affect – common in clients with developmental trauma. Her vulnerability was present when discussing food and maternal dynamics, but her sexuality was initially protected by a wall of anger. This type of defense isn't resistance – it's survival. Joelle's sexual self had become armored by bravado, cloaked in cultural language about empowerment, but still deeply entwined with shame.

She is a young, attractive woman who works in a male-dominated industry. Part of her confidence at work comes from being able to "keep up with the guys," particularly in her overt interest in sex. She was proud of the fact that she never slept with anyone from work. It gave her a sense of power and control, knowing that she had the interest of many of her male colleagues, yet never giving in to any advances. This was in contrast to the casual sex she was having outside of work.

This tension between power and collapse is a hallmark of what some feminist theorists have called defensive sexuality – a performance of agency that overlays a lack of internal safety or consent. Joelle's work identity provided her with a structure in which to feel in control, but her personal relationships repeated a different pattern entirely.

Her biggest goal coming into therapy was to "stop hooking up" with men that she wasn't attracted to. She wanted to stop feeling obligated to have sex with someone simply because they were flirting with her or had bought her a few drinks. She felt like she was holding herself back from dating men that she might want a committed relationship with. She had a vision of the type of man she would want as a long-term romantic partner: someone who was successful, intelligent, and attractive. Having casual sex without any discernment wasn't helping Joelle meet the type of man she wanted to date.

This moment in the therapeutic arc is important. Joelle had not yet made contact with the deeper grief and trauma underlying her behavior, but she had identified a conflict between desire and behavior. Her values and her actions were misaligned – what the OCSB model sees as the crux of compulsive sexual behavior. Her stated goal – "I want to stop sleeping with men I'm not attracted to" – became the organizing principle for our work. But the deeper emotional terrain was only beginning to emerge.

Frameworks for Healing: Sex Addiction and OCSB

Before diving into Joelle's experience with these frameworks, it's worth pausing to clarify an important distinction.

While Joelle's behaviors might be described as "sex addiction" in some circles, it's important to distinguish between addiction and compulsion. Addiction models tend to frame the problem as a loss of control caused by biochemical dependency, often addressed through abstinence-based approaches. In contrast, compulsive sexual behavior is often an affect regulation strategy – an attempt to manage emotional distress, shame, or trauma through patterned action. As researchers such as Ley (2012), Prause and Ley (2017), and Kleinplatz (2012) argue, the language of addiction can sometimes obscure the symbolic and relational dimensions of sexual behavior, especially when it reinforces shame. In psychoanalytic sex therapy, we often interpret compulsive behavior as a communication – an expression of unmet needs or dissociated experience, rather than a disease state. For Joelle, this distinction became clinically useful: it allowed us to explore her behavior without pathologizing her desire. This theoretical distinction became deeply relevant during a turning point in Joelle's treatment.

During one session, Joelle arrived upset and reported that a friend suggested Joelle might have a sex addiction. Joelle found this an upsetting and humiliating characterization, but something about it resonated with her as well. There was a lot about her recent sexual behavior that felt out of her control. She didn't want to be having so much casual sex, yet somehow she couldn't set boundaries for herself. And she recognized that all the casual sex was interfering with her ability to start dating. And so during that session, she made the commitment to stop engaging in "drunken hookups." Instead, she decided to join a few dating apps and be more discerning about the men she went out with.

Joelle's ambivalence – feeling humiliated by the label of "sex addict," but also recognizing a lack of control – reflects the complexity of how compulsive sexual behavior shows up in the therapy room. For many clients, the term "addiction" can evoke intense shame and pathologization, even as they struggle with behaviors that feel unmanageable or self-defeating. As clinicians, our task is to help clients name what feels distressing without reinforcing a framework that reduces sexuality to disease or moral failure.

The idea of sex addiction is a controversial topic in the mental health field. The advocates for the sex addiction disease model see the sexual behavior as similar to other addictions, in that the person's relationship to sex has become pathological, that they have lost control over their sexual expression and that they have become powerless over their behavior. By accepting that they have become powerless and therefore accepting the label of an addict, the person can begin to recover from their sex addiction through a 12-step recovery model which is based on abstinence from the problematic behavior.

While this model has offered relief and structure to many, particularly those seeking containment from overwhelming compulsions, it also carries limitations. Unlike substances, sexuality is not something one can eliminate from life. And for many, including Joelle, the notion of abstinence from sexual expression felt more like punishment than empowerment.

Similar to an eating disorder or other process addictions, becoming abstinent to food or sex is not a realistic or achievable goal. And yet in many ways, this does accurately describe Joelle's current behavior and her relationship to her sexuality in that she felt without the power or control to say no.

At the same time, Joelle's reaction to the label "sex addict" marked an important turning point. While the term felt shaming to her, it also forced her to pause and reflect. For many clients, particularly those prone to denial, rationalization, or grandiosity, the confrontation inherent in the addiction model can be a necessary jolt – a way to cut through intellectual defenses and name a pattern that is truly unmanageable. In Joelle's case, although she initially rejected the label, it helped bring her attention to the repetitive nature of her sexual behavior and the toll it was taking on her life.

As a clinician, I've found that both the sex addiction model and the OCSB framework have value, depending on the individual. Clients who are consumed by shame, who feel defective or morally broken, often respond better to the compassionate, sex-positive orientation of the OCSB model. It gives them a way to reframe their behavior without collapsing into self-hatred. On the other hand, clients who operate with defenses rooted in denial, entitlement, or emotional avoidance may benefit from the clear structure and direct accountability of the sex addiction framework. The label itself can serve as a reality check – an organizing principle that interrupts chaos.

Rather than viewing these models as oppositional, I see them as different therapeutic entry points. Each one offers a language for making sense of OCSB, and the clinician's job is to assess which language best supports the client's emotional readiness, defenses, and capacity for change.

An alternative to the sex addiction model is the concept of OCSB, which shifts the focus away from the person as having an illness or disorder (the addict) and directs the focus on the problematic sexual behavior that the person experiences as out of control. The OCSB model, developed by Douglas Braun-Harvey and Michael Vigorito (2016), centers the misalignment between one's sexual values and one's behavior. It defines the problem not as an addiction, but as a breakdown in sexual health and congruence.

The OCSB model tends toward a more sex-positive, non-pathologizing lens, offering sexual health and satisfaction as a foundation for change. It helps clients identify what kind of sex they want to be having – and what's getting in the way. In this approach, the goal is not abstinence, but sexual integrity, defined by the alignment of behavior, desire, boundaries, and values.

Sex therapy is useful in creating an open and curious dialogue about sexual health, sexual functioning, and sexual satisfaction, along with the potential conflicts (erotic or otherwise) or compulsive sexual behavior that interfere with sexual health.

This model gave Joelle a framework to understand her experience that was neither shaming nor reductive. She could begin to see that her behavior wasn't the problem – it was a symptom of a deeper disconnection from her own desire, boundaries, and emotional needs. And therapy would provide a space not only to explore that disconnection but also to build a new foundation for sexual expression that felt safe, sovereign, and self-defined.

Exploring Sexual History and Scripts

A core component of sexual health is having an understanding and acceptance of who we are sexually. This develops from exploring and having a curiosity in our sexual selves. And yet our sexual selves are a complex web of bio-psycho-social factors that morph and shift as we develop over the lifespan. Sex therapist and author Suzanne Iasenza, in her book *Transforming Sexual Narratives*, writes about the significance of a client's sexual history in identifying both conscious and unconscious narratives. The sexual history is part of an overall fluid and loose exploration of a client's sexual development as it relates to early childhood, adolescence, adulthood, societal influences, and current functioning.

What is unique about the sexual history is that we are looking more closely at how these factors shape the meaning of sexual experience and inviting clients to be reflective about the connections. For example, Joelle began to get curious about this feeling that she was never wanted. We explored when that feeling began, and she made the connection to her parents' divorce and feeling caught between her father's emotional withdrawal and her mother's emotional flooding.

She wondered if there was a connection between feeling that she was never wanted and not being able to regulate her sexual appetite. She asked, "Am I binging on sex to fill this void?"

This moment marked a subtle but important shift in our work. Joelle was beginning to symbolize what had previously been enacted. Her question was more than intellectual – it was a glimmer of insight that her sexual behavior might carry emotional meaning. In psychoanalytic terms, this reflects an early movement from repetition to representation, a capacity to hold contradiction, ask questions, and make links between past and present experience.

Another aspect of the sexual history is taking a close look at current sexual functioning and understanding what a person's sexual script is. The sexual script is the way that a person typically engages in a sexual experience, which can include both physical and psychological components.

Joelle initially thought that she had very little control over her sexual script, since she was so unselective about her sexual partners. But I probed a little deeper. When you notice someone begin to flirt with you at the bar, what kind of reaction are you having? Are you feeling anything in your body? Are you having any thoughts?

Joelle described an automatic reaction that happened every time. She would feel a mix of fear and anger. Fear because she didn't want to feel obligated to have sex with this person, and anger that he was flirting with her in the first place. The anger was connected to the feeling that it was an intrusion for him to initiate conversation with her, and the fear linked to the lack of control she felt over the outcome. Then a mental shift would occur – an acceptance of what she perceived was bound to happen – and it became a kind of game to Joelle, to feed into his attraction. The anger was still there, but the fear would turn into power.

This mix of feelings would cycle through her repeatedly throughout the evening: fear, anger, power. It wasn't until sex was over and the person was gone that the shame and disgust would set in.

This description reflects the emotional choreography of what Freud called compromise formation – a solution the psyche unconsciously devises to manage internal conflict. Joelle's sexual script held competing desires: the wish to feel wanted, the fear of being used, the defense of asserting control, and the residue of dissociation. Her shifting states – fear, anger, arousal, shame – could be seen as unintegrated self-states (Fisher, 2021), activated in rapid succession without reflective processing. These emotional loops are often embedded in compulsive sexual behaviors, where the behavior itself becomes the regulator of affect.

At one point, I asked Joelle if there was anything about the sexual experience that was physically enjoyable or satisfying to her. Her response was a look of confusion. Upon reflection, Joelle noted that she wasn't feeling much of anything in her body. She wasn't actually sure if she was having an orgasm or not. She did like to take control of the sex and prided herself on being able to bring the man to orgasm. She described it as a perverse victory.

Here we see another layer of the erotic script: Joelle could not locate pleasure within herself but could derive value through performance. Her sexual worth was externally anchored – validated by what she could provide, not by what she could feel. From a sex therapy perspective, this suggested the need for body-based interventions and a slowing down of the sexual process so that Joelle could begin to experience herself as a subject of pleasure, not just an object of arousal.

Exploring Joelle's sexual script is an intervention that combines both psychoanalytic therapy and sex therapy. It is not often that we are given an opportunity to talk about our experience of sex in a way that invites curiosity and self-awareness. Sex therapists bring a level of comfort, inquisitiveness, and knowledge of sex to the therapy experience that can be quite therapeutic in and of itself. There is an acceptance of sexual experience and the underlying feelings of shame that often accompany sex, particularly if there is a negative sexual symptom.

For many people, sex therapy is the first time talking about their sexual history or sexual preferences. Normalizing this experience and providing a forum for discussion and exploration can often greatly reduce symptoms of anxiety and shame independent of behavioral interventions. Psychoanalysis allows a therapist to look more closely at the potential deeper conflicts of sexual problems. What is the person's experience of sex and why? What is the context? How is this conflict or problem potentially connected to family-of-origin dynamics?

For Joelle, sex had become a way to fill an emotional void in herself, much in the same way her eating disorder had functioned. In sex, she could feel powerful and in control. It functioned as a way to distance herself from her emotional vulnerability. And at the same time, she was unconsciously repeating emotional wounds from childhood.

She projected onto the "random men at the bars" all the unlovable and unworthy parts of herself. Her casual sex encounters were mostly with people she wasn't attracted to, yet she felt an obligation to have sex with them anyway. This generated both anger and shame, rage and humiliation, overstimulation and dissociation.

This emotional and sexual cycle can be interpreted as a repetition compulsion. Having an understanding of relational psychodynamics can be profoundly useful in sex therapy, as many sexual symptoms and problems are rooted in relational trauma and can be understood as an unconscious message that the body holds. Exploring both Joelle's sexual script as well as the underlying family-of-origin psychodynamics allowed for a slowing down of the unconscious compulsive cycle, enough so that a behavioral modification could be introduced.

This twofold, integrated process is an essential method of psychoanalytic sex therapy.

Shifting the Compulsion: Dating as New Repetition

For the first time in her life, Joelle had made a deliberate decision to join a few dating apps and avoid the neighborhood bars. And for the next year of therapy, Joelle went on many dates with a wide range of men. She couldn't seem to get enough. Although she felt much better about avoiding casual sex with people she wasn't attracted to, she had replaced the compulsiveness of casual sex with a compulsiveness toward dating.

She would have multiple dates over the course of a weekend. She found herself exclusively interested in men who were financially successful and generous. She would only accept a date if it included a high-end restaurant. The only drawback in her mind was that often the men were much older than her, and she found them to be unattractive.

She was still having sex without any discretion, but felt empowered by the luxury of the dates she was having and the gifts she was receiving. Finally, she was getting something in return for having sex. And for the time being, this was enough for Joelle.

Here, we see what might be described in relational psychoanalysis as defensive growth – a shift in behavior that seems healthier on the surface but is still infused with repetition and symbolic reenactment. Joelle was no longer accepting drinks at the bar and going home with strangers, but she had constructed a new transactional template: one in which sex was exchanged for status, comfort, and fantasy fulfillment. In both dynamics, her agency remained conditional, rooted in her ability to fulfill someone else's desire while securing her own worth through external reward.

At least until she met Darren.

Darren was successful, attractive and charming. She didn't meet him on the dating app, but rather at a dinner event for work. She noticed him across the room and instantly felt attracted to him. This was a new feeling for her. They were introduced to each other and chatted most of the night. By the end of the event, Darren had suggested they get together for drinks and their first date was planned for later that week.

That first date quickly turned into a night of sex and by the end of the night, Joelle was having fantasies of a life together with Darren. It was the first time Joelle felt romantically interested in someone and she was swept away by the intensity of her feelings. Joelle was flushed with excitement as she described this first evening together in her session that week.

This shift – from casual sex to idealized romance – didn't mark the end of the repetition cycle. It marked its next phase. The emotional urgency Joelle experienced wasn't just about attraction; it was a rapid activation of unconscious longing. As analysts like Nancy McWilliams and Joyce McDougall have noted, sudden romantic intensity often conceals disso-ciated dependency needs and fears of abandonment. Joelle's fantasy of partnership was both an authentic desire and a defense against the deeper vulnerability of wanting to be seen and chosen.

One part of me felt happy for Joelle in her excitement and enthusiasm. Another part of me felt cautious and concerned by the rapid intensity of her excitement. Rather than mirror her excitement uncritically or dampen it too quickly, I chose to stay curious and engaged, using my concern as a cue to gently re-enter the sexual narrative with more focus on her. These moments – when the client rushes toward idealization or magical thinking – often mark a return to early relational templates. Staying grounded as a clinician allows the fantasy to unfold without foreclosing its meaning.

When I asked how the sexual experience was for her, she quickly said it was all great, that "Darren had an amazing body and had come three times in the course of the night." "Wonderful," I said and before she could change the subject, I quickly added, "And how was it for you?"

Joelle gave me a look and took a quick sigh. I could tell she was strug-gling with something. It had been just over a year of therapy with Joelle, and I knew she trusted me and felt supported by me. While I might not have pushed her under different circumstances, there was something about her facial expression that gave me concern.

"Why don't we talk through the sexual experience to get a better under-standing of what it was like for you?" I asked. She let out another sigh, this time a bit deeper and heavier.

"I really don't want this to turn into a negative thing, okay?" Joelle said. "I'll tell you, but don't lecture or judge me like my friend Debbie did," she continued.

"Therapists aren't allowed to be judgmental, so you are safe with me," I joked. Humor here served a specific function – it softened the shame while reestablishing safety. Rather than interrogate or interpret prematurely, I chose to follow her lead while keeping my protective instincts engaged. In moments when clients anticipate moral judgment, levity can disarm defensiveness and open the door to reflection.

She then proceeded to tell me that Darren was very much into anal sex, and he sees it as a sign of intimacy when a woman is willing to have anal sex.

"Oh okay. So you had anal sex with him, is that right?" I asked.

She responded, "Yeah and it was really hot. I liked it a lot. My friend Debbie thought it was sleazy for him to go for that on our first date, but I'm fine with it. I feel super close to him and I can really see myself falling for him. He is the first guy that I can actually imagine being with long term. We spent a lot of the night talking about our ideas around marriage and commitment."

In keeping with my promise to not be judgmental, I responded, "Okay, great. It sounds like you are happy to be feeling so excited about him. That is a new experience for you and I can see how you would be excited." I continued, "And was that your first time having anal sex? Did he use protection? Was there any discomfort for you? Is there anything that would be helpful regarding anal sex to talk about?"

She responded that it was all good and there wasn't anything more to talk about, except that she hoped they would be having lots of anal sex in the future and that she loved it.

At that moment, I felt protective of Joelle. I could tell that she was in "tough girl" mode and wasn't going to budge in her positive perception of the sexual experience with Darren, even though it didn't sound genuine. She seemed to be trying hard to convince me – and maybe herself too – that having anal sex for the first time, and on a first date, was perfectly reasonable.

This interaction reflected the subtle complexity of the transference. Joelle wanted me to validate her sense of empowerment, but there was also a fragile part of her that didn't yet feel ready to be examined too closely. The erotic encounter with Darren may have felt "hot," but the emotional velocity – the idealization, the defensiveness, the rush to commitment – suggested we were still inside the repetition, just wearing new clothes.

Countertransference Reactions

From the beginning, my countertransference reaction to Joelle had been dualistic. I had experienced her as both vulnerable and strong. Her strength could be understood as a defense against her vulnerability. Or rather, it was a protective strategy that had enabled her to cope with deep sadness and fear that she is "never enough."

This polarity – resilient on the surface, abandoned underneath – is a common presentation in clients with early relational trauma. In analytic terms, Joelle's presentation evoked what might be described as a false self-adaptation (Winnicott, 1960), formed to maintain attachment to caregivers who were emotionally unavailable or invasive. Her sexual bravado wasn't a reflection of true empowerment; it was a shield against dependency and emotional need.

There was also fear that showed up in my countertransference experience, particularly around Joelle's behavior that seemed risky and impulsive. And thus, I oftentimes felt very protective of her, particularly when her vulnerability showed through, but also when she was tough and trying to project a wall of armor around herself.

These protective feelings were important to notice. At times, they may have reflected real concern for her safety, but they also risked veering into rescue fantasies – a common countertransference reaction when the therapist identifies with the client's wounded inner child. Staying attuned to this dynamic helped me remain grounded in therapeutic neutrality while still offering empathic care.

Her overt sexuality came across to me as an attempt to compensate for her self-doubt. Under the armor of sexual bravado was a vulnerable little girl who never felt loved, validated, or seen by her parents. I had to be careful to protect and support the vulnerable parts of her, while holding back the tendency to be critical, controlling, or judgmental around her behavior that often seemed impulsive, reckless, self-destructive, and out of control.

The tension between support and judgment, concern and overidentification, required careful countertransference monitoring. Joelle's internalized object world – composed of a distant father and an emotionally intrusive mother – was often projected into the therapy relationship. At times, I sensed she unconsciously positioned me as the idealized caregiver who might finally understand her. Other times, I risked becoming the critical, shaming voice she had internalized.

So how does one work with this countertransferential material? The first step is being aware of it. In my case, letting myself know and acknowledge the contradictory feelings I was having related to Joelle, as well as the discomfort I felt. One can then use the countertransference material to better understand the psychodynamics at play, both intrapsychically and interpersonally. This is at the heart of psychoanalytic treatment: using the transference/countertransference matrix to anchor the therapy.

Sex therapy techniques can be particularly helpful in broadening the scope of interventions used, particularly when incorporating the body through behavioral techniques. Joelle's sexuality was a central arena of both her suffering and her recovery. Staying close to the emotional meanings behind her behaviors – without collapsing into reactivity – was part of how I tried to hold the therapeutic frame.

When Joelle's brief relationship ended with Darren, she was devastated and filled with intense feelings of anger and sadness. I could feel the emotional whiplash – how quickly the fantasy of intimacy gave way to the familiar terrain of abandonment, betrayal, and self-blame. Her disappointment was raw, and her pain palpable.

As a therapist, I found myself again holding multiple truths: my concern for her safety, my respect for her strength, and my awareness of the deeper grief that her sexual behavior often concealed. Joelle's pain wasn't just about Darren – it was about being returned, again and again, to a place of emotional aloneness that was far older than this relationship.

The challenge moving forward would be how to help Joelle interrupt this cycle – not by shutting down her sexuality, but by creating space for a different kind of contact with her body, her boundaries, and her desire. The task would be to shift from acting out to tuning in, from reenacting the past to cultivating new internal experiences. The next phase of our work would ask her to risk something unfamiliar: slowing down, feeling more, and listening to what her body had to say.

Therapeutic Crisis and the Turn Toward Self-Pleasure

Joelle's relationship with Darren was short-lived and began to quickly disintegrate in negative ways after their first date and first night of sex. Darren was eager to get together for sex – particularly anal sex – but was mostly unavailable for anything else. After a few weeks, Darren confessed to Joelle that he was married.

Joelle put up a good front with Darren and acted like this didn't bother her; that she was also just in it for the sex. And perhaps in an attempt to convince herself of this, she started hanging out at the neighborhood bars and hooking up with men again. The binging on food quickly followed.

In therapy, she would emotionally collapse. She would oscillate between crying and raging for the entire session. She felt totally out of control with her behavior outside of therapy and totally out of control with her emotions inside therapy. I knew it was necessary to intervene, as I was beginning to worry about Joelle's behavior and level of functioning.

At this point in the treatment, the question wasn't whether Joelle's behavior was problematic – it clearly was. The clinical challenge was how to intervene in a way that didn't mirror the judgment or rejection she had internalized from early caregivers. A purely interpretive approach risked reinforcing her shame. A purely behavioral one might have missed the symbolic dimension of her compulsions.

As a psychoanalyst, I might have considered offering an interpretation: that her sexual behavior was an enactment of unresolved conflicts around self-worth and emotional hunger, and that the collapse she experienced with Darren repeated an earlier object relationship in which the promise of intimacy was met with abandonment and betrayal. And while this was true, interpretation alone was not enough.

Joelle's body was the stage where her psychological wounds were being reenacted. Her sexuality wasn't the problem – it was the place where her need for love, validation, and release had found a form. She was using sex to regulate unbearable affect, reenact early dynamics, and manage unconscious conflict. Her erotic life was burdened by too much history and too little agency.

In this moment, I chose to take a more active stance.

I interrupted one of her raging and crying spells by saying, "Joelle, I'm sorry for interrupting you, but I want you to try and calm down for a minute. Can you take a few deep breaths because there is something that I want to say to you."

Joelle looked at me startled, "What do you want to say?" she asked.

I knew this moment required careful balance – one where containment had to be paired with clarity. Rather than interpret the underlying meaning of her spiral, I chose a direct intervention grounded in our trust. When a client is overwhelmed by shame and dysregulation, insight can sometimes land as critique. But a well-timed boundary, paired with care, can create the space for emotional reset.

"You might not like hearing this, but I'm worried about you. You are drinking a lot and hooking up with men again. You are having anal sex with Darren and I'm not sure that you even enjoy that. Your binging has started again. I know you are angry that Darren wasn't honest about being married. And I know you are disappointed and sad about it. But we have to come up with another strategy here, because drinking, hooking up, and binging are only going to make you feel worse about yourself."

She let out a heavy sigh and said, "I know you are right, but I just don't know what else to do."

"I have an idea," I said, "but you are going to have to trust me a little on this one. Are you willing to give this a try?"

I asked Joelle to stop going to the bars and to stop having casual sex. I also asked her to end the affair with Darren. She agreed to both of these requests and joked that I was putting her on a sex detox. Joelle was partially correct – but not exactly. My idea was to help her reclaim her sexuality, not abstain from it. The goal wasn't withdrawal; it was redirection.

I then asked Joelle how she felt about masturbation and if she thought it might be helpful for her. I presented the idea of masturbation as an exercise in becoming curious about her body and her sexuality, outside of partnered sex or a relationship dynamic.

While this might seem like a behavioral suggestion, it was deeply rooted in both trauma theory and psychoanalytic practice. I was offering Joelle a transitional space – a Winnicottian middle ground – where her body could begin to symbolize rather than reenact. Solo sexual exploration allowed her to cultivate sensation without threat, and to locate pleasure outside of performance or approval. This was not just about arousal; it was about agency.

I presented the idea of masturbation as a practice in self-attunement. "What if your sexuality didn't have to be something that gets negotiated in relationship?" I asked. "What if it could be something that's just yours for a while?"

Joelle was intrigued. She admitted that she hadn't ever masturbated with any regularity and was curious about what the experience would be like. She was also ready to give casual sex a break. Together, we created a structure: Joelle would try masturbating several times a week, not with the goal of orgasm alone, but with the intention of becoming more familiar with what she enjoyed, what felt good, and how her body responded to touch. Joelle decided she would try masturbating several times a week to begin focusing on her own pleasure. Introducing this kind of somatic assignment required a delicate balance – offering structure without evoking performance pressure. I framed it not as a task to achieve, but as an experiment in self-listening. I also normalized the awkwardness of starting something unfamiliar, reminding her that exploration doesn't require mastery. By aligning the intervention with her readiness and agency, we kept the work grounded in choice rather than compliance.

I told her about *OMGYes*, a research-based website that offers instructional videos for women to learn about female pleasure, masturbation techniques, and orgasm. The clinical rationale behind this resource was twofold: to depathologize self-touch and to anchor the practice in a context of permission and empowerment. Rather than reinforcing the idea that sex needed to be relational, performative, or externally validated, this was about Joelle discovering what pleasure might mean when it was centered around *her*.

The Healing Journey: From Trauma Release to Pleasure

For the next couple of months, Joelle committed to her weekly masturbation practice and would talk about the experience in our sessions. It was the first time in her life that she was touching herself with any regularity. What emerged was not simply arousal – but emotional release. She described a visceral type of experience where she was crying and moaning throughout every masturbation session. There was much pain, hurt, humiliation, shame, and anger that was coming out. Joelle described not understanding why this happened but appreciated the opportunity to release all this emotion. She was exhausted after every masturbation experience.

Her body would intensely convulse during her orgasms, and afterward, her legs and torso would visibly shake for several minutes. During these convulsions, she would let out deep sounds that she described as moans. I understood this as Joelle releasing years' worth of relational trauma – stored not in declarative memory, but in the sensorimotor patterns of her nervous system.

From a somatic and trauma-informed lens, Joelle was experiencing what Peter Levine (1997) describes as *completing the defensive response* – allowing the body to do now what it could not do during the original experience of threat or violation. Her masturbation wasn't simply a sexual act; it was a process of trauma resolution through embodiment. The crying, shaking, and moaning were not pathological – they were signs that her nervous system was discharging what had been held in a frozen state.

A similar process unfolded in Connie's case, described in Chapter 5 (*Sexual Healing*), where her solitary masturbation practice became a site of emotional and physiological release. There, too, the body gave voice to what had once been unspeakable. While Connie's ritual held the symbolism of grief and rage, Joelle's masturbation journey began with dissociated pain and gradually moved toward sensuality, choice, and arousal. In both cases, the body led the way.

After about two months, Joelle started to report feeling more calm overall in her life. And the sessions were noticeably different – she was no longer as emotionally dysregulated. There were still regular moments of emotional flooding, but she was better able to recognize when this happened and talk through the feelings instead of becoming overwhelmed. Her affect was beginning to settle. She was developing affect tolerance, a foundational capacity in both trauma recovery and psychoanalytic growth.

Joelle also became more curious about her masturbation practice. She noticed that she wasn't crying during every experience. She began to experiment with different methods and techniques, paying attention to what she enjoyed and what her preferences were. She started to delay her orgasm in order to feel more pleasure in her body. She enjoyed having prolonged masturbation experiences focused not just on release, but on relaxation, exploration, and enjoyment.

In many ways, Joelle was rewriting her sexual script. Where sex had previously been rushed, performative, or dissociated, she was now learning to stay present with sensation. She was shifting from compulsive sexual discharge to conscious erotic engagement – from reenactment to regulation.

At this point in the therapy, I suggested the book *Sex for One: The Joy of Selfloving* by Betty Dodson, the noted sexologist and feminist author who writes about the healing and liberating power of masturbation. Dodson's work, grounded in both sex-positive feminism and body sovereignty, helped affirm that what Joelle was doing wasn't just therapeutic – it was radical. She was reclaiming the right to feel.

Around the same time, Joelle began to incorporate yoga into her exercise routine and found it both challenging and satisfying. Learning and practicing the yoga poses, challenging her endurance and strengthening her body felt both difficult and calming. She began to make connections between the mindfulness she was learning in her yoga classes and her masturbation experiences, where she was becoming more focused on her body and what pleasure felt like for her.

This integration of somatic practices – yoga, breath, embodied touch – strengthened her connection to herself. She was no longer seeking relief through dissociation. She was building the capacity to stay *with* herself in the moment.

She also began to have sexual fantasies that she incorporated into her masturbation. She found herself fantasizing about romantic encounters with men that led to passionate sex and lovemaking. She brought these fantasies into her masturbation experiences and found them to be highly sensual and arousing. She talked about discovering a new part of her sexuality through the fantasies: a part of her that was interested in romance and flirtation. She amusingly would refer to her fantasies as innocent and sweet.

During one therapy session, Joelle mused, "I never thought I would get turned on by romance or the idea of love making. But something happens when I am fantasizing about a man about to enter me and looking me in the eyes to tell me he loves me. It's like my whole body wants to open up to that. What used to be waves of emotional pain now feels like waves of longing and desire."

Joelle's words signaled something profound. Pleasure was no longer bound to pain. For the first time, her arousal was woven with tenderness, desire, and trust. She was imagining a sexual experience in which she was *seen*, *valued*, and *loved*. Her body – once a battleground of shame and survival – was becoming a site of connection, integration, and possibility.

Transformation and Integration

What struck me was how far Joelle had come – from acting out to act-ing with intention. She was no longer reacting from emotional overwhelm but choosing how she wanted to relate to her body, her pleasure, and her boundaries. Her sexuality had moved from being a site of repetition and reenactment to one of exploration and sovereignty.

Joelle eventually began dating again and had a very different experience this time around. She enjoyed the men she was dating and avoided going into the bars. She found herself more naturally meeting men in organic ways – through friends or yoga classes – and these connections felt more grounded. Sex became a more natural and enjoyable experience for her. She was more aware of her own body and her own sexual interests and preferences. She was able to guide a sexual experience to incorporate her desire, as well as her partner's desire.

This marks a significant shift from her earlier sexual scripts, which were dominated by dissociation, obligation, and performance. Now, she was able to inhabit her body and her desire more fully. Sex became an act of presence, not escape.

She described the evolution of her sexual style as becoming more pas-sionate, sensual, and erotic. It was more about connection and less about competition. And although she enjoyed the sexual encounters she was hav-ing, Joelle wasn't in a rush to enter into a committed or monogamous rela-tionship. She was enjoying her sexual freedom and emotional liberation. Her sexuality became a place of curiosity and pleasure for her. Sex was no longer linked to being drunk or binging on food. It didn't feel out of con-trol to her. She was appreciative of the sexual connections she was having with others, rather than feeling that sex was about conquest, proving her worth, or managing pain.

In analytic terms, Joelle had developed greater ego strength and affect regulation – capacities that allowed her to engage with her desire with-out being consumed by it. Her libidinal energy was no longer tied up in defensive enactments or self-punishment. She was now using her sexuality to build connection with herself and others. Pleasure had become not just something she *accessed*, but something she *allowed*.

A few weeks later, Joelle described an interaction she had with her mother that felt significant to her. She was traveling with her mother on a beach vacation, and her mother commented on how good Joelle's body looked. Joelle's immediate reaction was to become enraged. As she told the story in therapy, she began to cry. She said that it was both infuriating that her mother was still so focused on her body, and deeply sad that her mother couldn't seem to get past the surface. Even when trying to give a compliment, it still felt like a form of control.

Joelle didn't expect much more from her mother and, in part, had accepted her emotional limitations. But her sadness came from a deeper recognition: there had never been emotional attunement. Her mother had attended to Joelle's body, but not to Joelle's self. Her appearance was scrutinized, but her inner world was unseen.

Having an awareness of her mother's limitations – and the impact it had on her emotional development – was a profound shift. She was no longer acting out the relational trauma through her sexuality, but rather naming it and metabolizing the feelings. This movement from reenactment to narrative, from acting out to symbolic expression, is one of the most powerful transformations therapy can facilitate.

As a result, there was a clearing out of the trauma and an opportunity to experience pleasure and self-acceptance. Joelle had come to understand that her body was not just a site of seduction or betrayal – it was a source of wisdom, desire, and healing. The transformation in Joelle was nothing short of stunning – not because she had eliminated all symptoms, but because she had begun to live in relationship to herself.

Conclusion: The Integration of Psychoanalytic and Sex Therapy Interventions

The psychoanalytic interventions used in this case began with the conceptualization of the client's behavior as meaningful – a symbolic expression of unconscious emotional conflict rather than a moral failing or character flaw. I was listening not only to Joelle's words but to her enactments, her repetitions, and her emotional rhythms. What was being communicated through her compulsions? What deeper longings were encoded in her symptoms?

In Joelle's case, her sexuality had become the arena where early relational trauma was reenacted. Her feelings of low self-worth and shame were being repeated and reinforced through romantic and sexual experiences. The therapeutic task was not to shame her behavior or demand abstinence, but to help her recognize what her behavior was attempting to resolve – and to offer alternative ways of meeting those same emotional needs.

As Joelle began to speak more openly about the feelings underlying her sexual choices and connect them to her family-of-origin dynamics, she was able to slow down the cycle of compulsive reenactment. This allowed space for new behavior and new meaning to emerge. With more self-acceptance and curiosity, she began to explore what actually brought her pleasure, what kind of relationships she desired, and how she wanted to express her sexuality.

Throughout our work, psychoanalytic techniques such as mirroring, attunement, and exploring unconscious meanings were crucial in creating a therapeutic alliance strong enough to tolerate difficult material. These interventions supported the emergence of what Kohut referred to as the selfobject transference – in which the therapist becomes a stabilizing presence, allowing the client to gradually internalize new forms of self-regulation and self-worth.

At the same time, sex therapy interventions played a vital role in supporting Joelle's healing. Providing psychoeducation, normalizing masturbation, and offering structured behavioral exercises gave her a safe way to reconnect with her body. Tools like *OMGYes* and Betty Dodson's *Sex for One* were both valid educational resources, as well as bridges to self-attunement. The act of masturbating with curiosity and intention allowed Joelle to begin experiencing pleasure as something self-generated, not other-dependent.

This kind of integration – of psychoanalytic insight and sex therapy technique – is particularly important when working with clients like Joelle, whose sexuality is both a source of pain and a potential site of healing. A purely behavioral approach would have missed the deeper wounds driving her compulsions. A purely analytic stance might have failed to offer her the tools she needed to reconnect with her body.

By combining both, we were able to help Joelle move from a cycle of compulsion and collapse to a state of greater coherence. Her transformation extended beyond her sexual life into her broader capacity for emotional regulation, embodied presence, and authentic connection.

This case illustrates how sexual behavior often serves as both symptom and solution – a maladaptive attempt to soothe unresolved pain that paradoxically reinforces it. When clinicians create space for clients to reflect on the unconscious meanings of their sexual behaviors, while also providing tools to explore new experiences of pleasure, agency, and embodiment, profound healing becomes possible.

Through this integrated approach, Joelle was able to reclaim her sexuality not as a problem to be fixed, but as a path toward emotional repair, erotic vitality, and relational freedom.

Summary of Key Concepts

- **Out-of-control sexual behavior (OCSB)** can be understood not solely as impulsivity or addiction, but as a symbolic expression of unresolved relational trauma and unmet emotional needs.
- **Repetition compulsion** – first described by Freud – helps explain how individuals unconsciously recreate early relational wounds in their adult sexual lives, seeking mastery through reenactment but often reinforcing the original pain.

- A **non-pathologizing, integrated treatment approach** draws from both psychoanalytic theory and sex therapy practice, supporting insight while offering concrete tools for behavioral change and sexual health.
- **Sexual scripts** – the patterns and expectations that govern one's sexual behavior – reveal internalized beliefs about agency, worth, and connection. Exploring these scripts can illuminate unconscious dynamics and open the door to transformation.
- **Solo sexual practices,** especially masturbation, can function as somatic reprocessing when approached with mindful intention. When clients begin to notice what emerges emotionally and physically during self-touch, the body becomes a site of narrative, not just stimulation.
- **Emergent romantic and emotional fantasies** – especially those that arise during mindful masturbation – can offer valuable insight into a client's evolving erotic identity. Rather than interpreting these as symptoms, clinicians can explore them as signs of increased emotional integration and capacity for intimacy.
- **Therapeutic integration** – of psychoanalytic interpretation, relational attunement, behavioral interventions, and sex-positive education – offers a multidimensional path for healing compulsive or painful sexual behavior.

For Clinical Reflection

- When a client presents with sexual behavior that feels compulsive or out of control, how do you understand the function of the behavior? Are you more inclined to see it through a trauma lens, an addiction model, or both?
- How do you hold and work with your own countertransference when a client describes behavior that is impulsive, risky, or emotionally dysregulated?
- In your practice, how comfortable are you exploring a client's sexual script in detail? Are there aspects of fantasy, arousal, or masturbation that you find difficult to explore? If so, what might those discomforts reveal?
- Can you distinguish between a client's sexual behavior as self-harming versus self-soothing? How does your clinical stance shift based on that distinction?
- Are there ways in which your theoretical orientation privileges insight over embodiment – or vice versa? How might you integrate both in your approach?
- How do you assess when it is appropriate to offer structured behavioral interventions in the context of psychodynamic work?

Chapter 8

More Than the Agreement
Love, Loss, and Boundaries in Consensual Non-Monogamy

Understanding Consensual Non-Monogamy in Therapy

Consensual non-monogamy (CNM) represents a broad and diverse range of relational structures – from polyamory and open relationships to relationship anarchy and solo polyamory. While these configurations have become increasingly visible in contemporary culture, they remain undertheorized in traditional psychoanalytic discourse. Historically, psychoanalysis often viewed non-monogamy through a pathologizing lens, interpreting it as a defense against intimacy, an expression of unresolved oedipal dynamics, or a sign of narcissistic disturbance. But such formulations fail to capture the richness, intentionality, and emotional complexity that many people bring to their non-monogamous relationships.

Contemporary relational psychoanalysis, with its emphasis on mutual recognition, intersubjectivity, and the fluidity of desire, offers a more expansive framework. As Jessica Benjamin (1990) articulates, the core tension in all relationships lies in the dynamic between connection and autonomy – the desire to be fully seen by another without losing one's separateness. This tension, echoed in Tammy Nelson's (2013) work on reimagining fidelity and commitment, is not eliminated in CNM – it is often intensified. Nelson argues that even when couples step outside traditional monogamy, they still long for trust, honesty, and shared meaning – qualities that must be actively cultivated regardless of structure.

Rather than viewing CNM as an alternative to monogamy, it can be more accurately understood as a relational amplifier – one that makes visible the emotional negotiations that all intimate relationships must contend with. The polyamorous frame invites multiple attachment figures, which can simultaneously evoke security and destabilization. From an attachment-based perspective, as Jessica Fern (2020) emphasizes in *Polysecure*, secure functioning in non-monogamy requires not only transparent

DOI: 10.4324/9781003318187-9

agreements but also a capacity to tolerate emotional complexity, regulate reactivity, and integrate multiple forms of intimacy.

In this sense, agreements in CNM relationships are not merely behavioral contracts; they are emotional boundaries that symbolize mutual care, trust, and containment. When those agreements shift or break down, as in the case that follows, the psychological impact can mirror that of betrayal, loss, or reactivation of childhood attachment injuries. CNM couples do not just need communication skills – they need emotional literacy, internal regulation, and the ability to tolerate ambivalence, especially when relational desires evolve in conflicting directions.

In my clinical work with CNM clients, I have found that the most profound therapeutic work often emerges not from discussing logistics or negotiating calendars, but from exploring the unconscious meanings embedded in the structure of their agreements. What does it mean to "belong" to more than one person? How does one hold loyalty in multiplicity? What fantasies, fears, or inherited scripts get activated when boundaries are stretched, renegotiated, or violated?

The following case study explores these tensions in depth, highlighting how CNM can support emotional vitality – but also how it can expose unresolved grief, ambivalence, and the fragility of even long-standing relational bonds. Through a psychoanalytic lens, we will examine how unconscious conflict, shifting attachment needs, and the complexity of erotic differentiation shaped this triadic configuration over time.

Case Overview and Relationship Mapping

Malina arrived at my office with her secondary partner Cheryl. They had just spent the weekend together and carried the intoxicating glow of mutual adoration. Cheryl, visiting from Colorado, cherished these bimonthly NYC weekends – not only to reconnect with Malina but to feel a sense of aliveness she missed since moving away ten years prior. The stated reason for the appointment was to address some difficult emotions Cheryl was experiencing in their relationship. But underneath this, something deeper was shifting – something that neither woman was quite ready to acknowledge.

Cheryl and Malina had met 15 years ago in law school. Their connection began as a friendship – a mutual recognition of being gay women in a predominantly heterosexual environment – but quickly deepened into a romantic and sexual bond. From the beginning, Cheryl was clear: she identified as solo polyamorous and did not anticipate ever having a primary partner. She valued her independence and autonomy, and she envisioned a life unconstrained by conventional relational obligations.

Malina, in contrast, had always imagined herself marrying and having children. That wasn't an immediate goal – she was immersed in the intensity of law school – but she held that vision for her future. At the time, Cheryl's polyamorous identity didn't feel threatening. Malina didn't see Cheryl as her eventual life partner; she was drawn instead to the depth of their emotional connection and the comfort of their shared values. In the safety of that mutual understanding, their relationship thrived.

From a psychoanalytic perspective, one could say that their relational frame – friendship at the core, romance as a shared adventure – created a transitional space where each could safely explore intimacy without the pressure of convergence. The relationship structure allowed both women to hold on to vital parts of themselves while still remaining emotionally tethered. The boundaries were clear and the roles consensual.

Over time, Cheryl occasionally dated other women, and Malina didn't experience jealousy. Their non-monogamy worked well for them both. Cheryl supported Malina's exploration of other relationships, even encouraging her when she met Bea, a woman she began dating seriously. Cheryl, still planning to move to Denver, believed that Bea could offer Malina the kind of life partnership she herself never sought.

At this point, I met all three – Malina, Cheryl, and Bea – for the first time. They had come to therapy to clarify the visions of their future. Malina was leaning toward ending her relationship with Cheryl to honor her growing commitment to Bea. She wanted monogamy, marriage, and children. While she deeply loved Cheryl, she feared that maintaining the relationship could jeopardize Bea's trust and the exclusivity she now craved.

However, Bea's response was surprising and unexpected. She valued Malina's willingness to set boundaries for the sake of their relationship – it reassured her of Malina's loyalty – but she also felt uneasy being the reason that Cheryl and Malina would split. As the child of high-conflict divorced parents, Bea carried deep ambivalence about being the cause of someone else's pain. Her parents' joint custody arrangement had made her feel like a burden, and the thought of disrupting Cheryl and Malina's connection triggered echoes of that old guilt.

Here, the psychoanalytic theme of triangulation is unavoidable. Bea, like many children of divorce, had internalized the fantasy that her presence disrupted the parental dyad. Now, as an adult, she found herself caught in a familiar triangle – torn between wanting closeness and fearing the emotional costs of it. Her attachment history gave her a particular sensitivity to being the cause of relational rupture.

In a moment of insight and generosity, Bea suggested a compromise: that Cheryl and Malina continue seeing each other bimonthly for weekend visits. It was a move that surprised all of us. Cheryl felt seen and prioritized in a way she hadn't expected. Her solo poly identity had often been met with skepticism or marginalization, but here was someone – Bea – honoring the emotional weight of her bond with Malina. Malina, in turn, felt a rush of gratitude toward Bea, whose open-heartedness only deepened her sense that this was the woman she wanted to build a family with.

And so, the agreement was born. Cheryl moved to Denver. Bea and Malina remained in New York, eventually marrying and having two children together. Over the next decade, their lives grew busy and layered. Cheryl occasionally reached out for individual sessions to process the challenges of her own relationships in Colorado, and Malina and Bea sometimes returned for couples work – navigating the shifting terrain of marriage, parenting, and career. Throughout it all, the bimonthly weekends between Cheryl and Malina continued.

These weekends came to function as what Winnicott might call a transitional space – a suspended reality, separate from their daily lives, but deeply sustaining. For Malina, they were an erotic and emotional oasis – a break from the demands of parenting and monogamy. For Cheryl, they preserved a sense of continuity and devotion. They reminisced about their law school years, rekindled their sexual connection, and re-entered a version of themselves that still lived in the rhythm of those early days.

But even the most thoughtful agreements can't account for emotional evolution. Over time, something began to shift.

Attachment, Fantasy, and Erotic Differentiation

Malina discovered a renewed sexual awakening with Cheryl, as they began to experiment with some light BDSM play together. Malina was experimenting with her submissive side and allowing Cheryl to guide her into some erotic fantasies of sensual control. The trust of their long friendship allowed Malina to go to vulnerable places within herself sexually that felt both intimidating and exciting.

In many ways, this speaks to how erotic vitality often emerges not in spite of safety, but because of it. As Stephen Mitchell and others in the relational school have noted, eroticism thrives in the paradox between security and freedom. With Cheryl, Malina could access a part of her sexual self that had remained dormant – tucked beneath the layers of routine, caregiving, and the emotional responsibilities of family life. The relationship served as a space where previously inaccessible fantasies could be safely explored.

In retrospect, Malina acknowledged that something was starting to shift emotionally for her at this point. She was becoming more elusive with Bea and avoided telling her about the new sexual play with Cheryl. She found herself fantasizing about sex with Cheryl more often and drifting into day-dreams about their next weekend away.

Cheryl too felt the increasing intensity of their connection, but in different ways. After more than a decade of solo polyamory, Cheryl was beginning to yearn for a more consistent relationship structure. She had recently begun exploring what it might feel like to have a primary partner – something she had previously rejected. A woman she dated in Denver had briefly taken on that role, but it was Cheryl's connection with Malina that felt most emotionally fulfilling.

This shift reflects a deeper relational evolution that neither of them had planned for. Cheryl's desire for primacy reflected a growing need to be integrated more fully into Malina's daily life. From a psychoanalytic standpoint, Cheryl's longing wasn't just about frequency of contact – it was about recognition, belonging, and an emerging desire to be part of Malina's inner circle, not just her erotic periphery. Her emotional investment in Malina had reached a point where the structure of their existing agreement no longer matched her internal experience.

At the same time, Malina's deepening sexual connection with Cheryl reflected something more than novelty – it was a space of erotic differentiation. As David Schnarch describes, sexual differentiation allows one to maintain a solid sense of self while remaining emotionally close to another. Cheryl had become someone with whom Malina could explore a part of herself that she hadn't yet accessed within her marriage. It was not a replacement for Bea, but a contrast – an expansion of her erotic self.

And yet, the more Cheryl and Malina explored this terrain together, the more complicated it became. Their growing closeness was no longer fully in alignment with the structure they had previously agreed upon. What had once been openly acknowledged had now become partially hidden. Malina and Cheryl both began to feel the pull of secrecy, guilt, and ambivalence.

They were crossing boundaries, and they both knew it. But neither was ready to give it up. For the first time in their long relationship, what each of them wanted – and what each of them was willing to risk – was no longer aligned.

Boundaries, Secrecy, and Conflict

And so for the next several months, Malina and Cheryl considered what this would be like and whether it was possible. Malina kept all this information private from Bea, as she was certain Bea would not be accepting or interested in a reconfiguring of their agreement. Over the years, Bea had occasionally become jealous of Malina's time away from the family to meet with Cheryl. She had herself considered finding an occasional lover but quickly gave up the idea because the logistics of that seemed too complicated and unnecessarily stressful on their family life. But it did create some resentment – that Malina was able to indulge in ways Bea didn't give herself permission to.

Malina and Cheryl both felt guilty about this sexual and emotional secrecy they kept from Bea, yet both of them found it too meaningful to want to give up. Their relationship, which had once been openly acknowledged within the structure of Bea and Malina's marriage, now carried a charge of something unsanctioned. In this way, it began to resemble an affair – not in structure, but in emotional tone. Their agreement, once clear and mutual, was quietly unraveling.

From a relational standpoint, the secrecy functioned as a defense – against disruption, confrontation, and loss. Both Cheryl and Malina avoided speaking openly with Bea, not only to protect her but to protect the fragile container that held their own evolving connection. In psychoanalytic terms, the shared avoidance created a kind of collusion: a mutual fantasy space where desire could continue to flourish without the threat of external reality.

Cheryl pushed to renegotiate the boundaries with Bea, hoping that Bea would be open to having a more balanced polyamorous relationship where Malina would spend equal amounts of time with Bea and Cheryl. Malina pushed back, not feeling ready to introduce this idea to Bea, knowing that it would create conflict and tension between them and not wanting to jeopardize the stability of her family life.

Over the years, Malina had sensed Bea's slight resentment of their arrangement. It was never enough that either needed to discuss it at length, and because their lives were busy, full, and satisfying as they raised their children together, it remained in the background. But their emotional and sexual communication had waned. What had once been a space of thoughtful engagement – where Bea and Malina reflected on how Cheryl's presence opened up new insights about attachment, family-of-origin dynamics, and erotic individuality – had narrowed into silence.

In the earlier stages of their non-monogamy, the shared agreement had actually fueled intimacy. It brought Bea and Malina into deeper emotional contact and provided a structure for open reflection. But over time, and with the pressures of parenting, work, and routine, that structure became more symbolic than lived. The consent had gone unrenewed. And in its place, avoidance and assumption had taken hold.

Despite feeling guilty about her lack of transparency, Malina preferred to keep things intact. She wanted to continue exploring this sexual side of herself with Cheryl, yet wasn't ready or willing to potentially destabilize her family life with Bea.

Here we begin to see the emotional and structural limits of the original agreement. The concept of "negotiated non-monogamy" often assumes that all partners will remain static in their desires, boundaries, and relational needs – but in practice, these needs evolve. As Jessica Fern (2020) notes in *Polysecure*, agreements require continual re-attunement, especially when attachment bonds are shifting. Without this, the agreements themselves can become brittle – more of a relic than a living document.

For Cheryl and Malina, the cost of not renegotiating became increasingly apparent. Their relational energy, once enlivening and connective, was now infused with anxiety, secrecy, and tension. The emotional infrastructure could no longer bear the weight of what the relationship had become.

The Breakdown of Agreements

This created tension between Cheryl and Malina for the first time in their relationship. They requested some joint sessions to talk through their differing needs and try to come to an agreement on how to move forward. Cheryl felt strongly in her desire for a more consistent relationship and didn't want to compromise on that. Solo poly no longer satisfied her in the way it had previously done, and she didn't like the feeling that her changing relationship with Malina was now becoming secretive and hidden from Bea. This felt like a compromise she could no longer maintain.

For Cheryl, what had once felt like freedom now felt like fragmentation. Her solo poly identity had always provided her with autonomy and emotional sovereignty – but now, with Malina, she longed for relational continuity, acknowledgment, and shared direction. In relational terms, her attachment system had reorganized. What had once been a structure of abundance – multiple partners, multiple homes – now felt dispersed and disconnected. She wasn't asking Malina to choose, but she was asking her to step more fully into mutuality.

For the first time, Cheryl had thoughts of ending her relationship with Malina. It was too painful to want more and feel like she was unable to fully embrace that. She was surprised at her longing to have a primary relationship, but this is where her heart was taking her, and it felt like an important calling to follow.

Malina, on the other hand, was devastated at the thought of ending their long history together and craved more sexual exploration with Cheryl. It was the trust and safety of their long relationship that allowed Malina to embrace this more vulnerable part of her sexuality. She wasn't confident that it could emerge within her relationship with Bea. And yet, the thought of revealing to Bea what was developing between her and Cheryl felt too threatening for her to consider.

She respected Bea and, more than anything, valued the family they had built together. It felt too selfish to ask Bea's permission for more leniency in their non-monogamy agreement. Her life had been built with Bea, and it didn't seem fair to invite Cheryl into an equal partnership when that was not what they had originally agreed to. And Malina didn't experience the same need as Cheryl for their relationship to evolve into an equal primary structure. As Tammy Nelson (2013) argues in *The New Monogamy*, relational agreements are not fixed promises but evolving documents shaped by emotional development, shifting priorities, and changing life stages. Nelson's framework invites therapists to help clients explore whether their agreements are still serving the relationship, rather than simply policing boundaries. In this case, Cheryl's evolving needs pointed to a deeper misalignment between structure and feeling – one that required more than behavioral negotiation; it required a recognition of relational grief.

Here, we can see how the limitations of structure begin to press against the evolution of feeling. In early stages of non-monogamy, boundaries and agreements serve as scaffolding – they create safety, clarity, and mutual understanding. But over time, emotional bonds may deepen in ways that outgrow the original structure. When these shifts aren't acknowledged, avoidance often replaces negotiation. Malina's guilt about withholding information from Bea was not just about dishonesty – it was about a dissonance between her lived experience and her stated values.

From a psychoanalytic perspective, this is a classic intrapsychic conflict between duty and desire, between self-protection and emotional truth. Malina's reluctance to bring her evolving relationship with Cheryl into consciousness with Bea reflects the ambivalence that so often accompanies change. She didn't want to disrupt the stability she had worked so hard to build. Yet the emotional reality of her connection with Cheryl was no longer peripheral – it was central.

Cheryl, for her part, could no longer inhabit the margins. Her desire for emotional reciprocity, structural clarity, and equal footing was not a demand. For her, it was a declaration of growth. She was no longer the woman she had been 15 years ago, and neither was Malina. But their agreement had remained static.

What began as a relational structure rooted in love and mutual respect had reached its limits – not because anyone failed, but because love had changed.

Termination and Therapeutic Mourning

And so it was a painful process for Malina and Cheryl to recognize that they had reached a crossroads in their long relationship together. Neither of them wanted to end things, but they were no longer aligned in what they needed from one another. Cheryl felt herself moving toward a new phase of life – one that included stability, consistency, and mutual prioritization. Malina, in contrast, felt tethered by loyalty to the life she had built with Bea and their children. The divergence was an existential one and not simply logistical.

Malina experienced deep mourning and grief at the thought of saying goodbye to Cheryl, yet she knew that it was what Cheryl needed in order to move forward. She also knew, at least unconsciously, that something had shifted in her own emotional architecture – something she wasn't quite ready to reconfigure within her marriage. There was still a part of her that longed for the erotic vitality, the playfulness, the experimentation that she experienced with Cheryl. But she also felt a strong protectiveness over her family life and wasn't willing to jeopardize that stability, even for a love as enduring as hers and Cheryl's.

Over the next few months, they began the emotionally painful experience of saying goodbye to each other. In our joint sessions, they reflected on their long history together, shared their deep appreciation and love for one another, and grieved the ending – not just of their connection, but of the container that had held it for so many years.

From a psychoanalytic standpoint, the mourning process was layered and complex. As Freud wrote in his seminal essay *Mourning and Melancholia* (1917), mourning is the process by which we gradually withdraw emotional investment from a lost object. But what happens when the object we are mourning is not just a person, but a shared identity? A version of self, a version of possibility, a version of love? Cheryl and Malina were not only saying goodbye to each other – they were saying goodbye to the part of themselves that lived in the relational field they had co-created.

In these final sessions, the therapeutic task was to hold space for this rupture with care and dignity. Grief, when witnessed and honored, can become a form of integration. They told stories about their law school days, about the early nights of courtship, about the ways their friendship had grown into love. They remembered the risks they had taken to stay connected, and the generosity that had shaped their agreement. In doing so, they affirmed that their relationship was not a failure. It had lived, evolved, and now it was ending – not from neglect, but from truth.

After 15 years, they said goodbye – not only to each other but also to a relationship structure that had served as an emotional pillar in both of their lives. In its absence, something else would eventually emerge. But for now, the work was to grieve what had been.

As clinicians, we are often called to hold space for this kind of relational transition. In consensual non-monogamy, endings may carry particular weight, as partners part not because they no longer love one another, but because the structural fit no longer holds. Our role is to honor the depth of the attachment, help partners metabolize the loss, and support the ongoing integration of what that relationship offered.

Best Practices for Working with CNM Clients

The case of Malina, Cheryl, and Bea highlights how relational needs and identities evolve over time, often in ways that partners cannot anticipate when initially establishing agreements. What worked beautifully for Cheryl and Malina during their law school years – and even for the first decade of their bimonthly arrangement – eventually became insufficient as their relational needs shifted. The case illustrates the reality that sometimes even the most carefully constructed relationship agreements cannot accommodate all partners' needs indefinitely. The painful decision that Malina and Cheryl ultimately made – to end their relationship rather than continue in a configuration that didn't serve them both – reflects the courage required to recognize when a relational structure has reached its natural conclusion.

As Jessica Fern (2020) emphasizes in *Polysecure*, securely navigating non-monogamous relationships often requires integrating attachment awareness with intentional communication and flexible agreements. This framework can help both clients and clinicians hold space for evolving emotional needs without defaulting to shame or failure. Similarly, Martha Kauppi (2021) stresses the importance of ongoing collaborative agreements in CNM – not as fixed contracts but as evolving dialogues. When those dialogues become stagnant or avoided, even the most well-intentioned structures can begin to erode.

Nelson (2013) also argues that therapists should not focus solely on whether agreements are being kept or broken, but on whether those agreements still reflect the emotional and relational reality of the people involved. Nelson's framework invites therapists to help clients explore whether their agreements are still serving the relationship, rather than simply policing boundaries. In this case, Cheryl's evolving needs pointed to a deeper misalignment between structure and feeling – one that required more than behavioral negotiation; it required a recognition of relational grief.

Not all cases in psychotherapy – particularly in sex therapy – unfold with the same intensity, duration, or structure. Some clients enter therapy in crisis and engage in a long-term, emotionally immersive process that reveals the layers of trauma, desire, and defense. Others, like Malina, Cheryl, and Bea, may use therapy more episodically: returning during transitional moments or when relational dynamics require containment, clarification, or renegotiation. Their case did not require a linear deep dive into intrapsychic material. Instead, the work became a space to reflect on evolving relational needs, honor attachment shifts, and metabolize grief as agreements began to falter.

In my own clinical practice, I've come to value this variety. I enjoy working in different registers – sometimes deep and sustained, other times brief and targeted – because it keeps the work alive, spontaneous, and responsive. But this flexibility also requires a deep commitment to ongoing self-reflection. As therapists, we must be vigilant about our own counter-transference, including the temptation to impose a depth-oriented agenda when it may not serve the client. It's easy to conflate our desire for complexity with the client's actual needs. True attunement means staying curious: not only about the client's inner world but also about our own motivations, limitations, and preferences as clinicians.

Just as there is no single correct way to structure a non-monogamous relationship, there is no singular right way to structure a therapeutic practice. Some clinicians work strictly within behavioral, somatic, or psychodynamic frames; others build hybrid models that evolve over time. What matters is not adhering to a fixed method, but being reflective about how and why we practice the way we do. Like any living system, a therapy practice benefits from ongoing self-examination: Is this structure serving both the client and the clinician? What's being protected? What's being expressed?

Countertransference, in this sense, extends beyond the clinical dyad. It can also emerge in our relationship to the work itself – how we structure our practice, the clients we attract, and the roles we find ourselves playing. Our personal needs – for depth, stability, stimulation, or validation – can subtly shape how we show up. Staying in touch with these internal dynamics is part of the ethical discipline of psychoanalytic sex therapy. It allows us to offer a frame that is both intentional and alive – clear enough to hold, flexible enough to adapt, and spacious enough to meet clients where they are.

By approaching these relationships with curiosity, therapists can help clients navigate the complex emotional terrain of loving multiple people in ways that foster growth, integrity, and authentic connection.

Summary of Key Concepts

- **Consensual non-monogamy (CNM)** is not a one-size-fits-all model but a dynamic relational structure that requires ongoing negotiation, communication, and self-awareness. The meaning and function of agreements evolve over time as partners' emotional needs and life circumstances shift.
- **Attachment styles** play a significant role in shaping how individuals manage autonomy, intimacy, and emotional boundaries within CNM structures. Even when agreements are clear, unconscious attachment needs may emerge and complicate relational dynamics.

- **Erotic differentiation** can emerge more clearly in CNM arrangements, where sexual and emotional selves are allowed distinct expressions across relationships. These differences can foster growth but also provoke anxiety and desire for restructuring.
- **Therapeutic work with CNM clients** requires attunement to both structure and feeling: honoring explicit agreements while also exploring implicit emotional needs, loyalties, fantasies, and fears.
- **Grief, mourning, and loss** are often overlooked dimensions of CNM when relational configurations change or end. Naming these feelings within therapy supports closure and integration.
- **Clinical flexibility** – in session structure, pacing, and depth – is often required when working with CNM clients. A therapist's own comfort with varying formats and evolving client needs can impact the therapeutic alliance and outcome.
- **Countertransference** includes not only responses to the client but also reactions to our own practice structures, professional identities, and therapeutic philosophies. Recognizing and working with these reactions is central to ethical, responsive clinical care.

For Clinical Reflection

- How do I hold space for different kinds of relationships – including CNM, monogamy, and more fluid configurations – without imposing my own preferences or assumptions?
- In what ways do I support or constrain erotic differentiation within my clinical work? How comfortable am I with clients exploring different sexual selves in different relational contexts?
- What is my own framework around grief and relational endings? How do I help clients process mourning when a non-monogamous configuration changes or dissolves?
- How flexible is my therapeutic frame? Am I clear with myself about when I prefer deep, sustained work versus brief or intermittent support? Do I leave space for clients to define how they want to use therapy?
- What needs – emotional, financial, or professional – do I bring into my relationship with my practice? How do these needs shape who I work with, how I work, or what I unconsciously encourage in the room?
- Do I have an awareness of when my desire for a client to "go deeper" might be more about my own need for engagement or meaning than their actual readiness or goals?

Chapter 9

Between Knowing and Not Knowing

A Story of Sexual Fluidity

Reframing Sexual Fluidity Through a Psychoanalytic Lens

Contemporary understandings of sexuality have evolved from earlier binary and fixed conceptualizations. Research on sexual fluidity has shown that for many individuals, attractions, behaviors, and identities can shift across time in response to relational contexts, emotional connections, and changing environments. These insights challenge the view of sexuality as static and unchanging, suggesting instead that erotic orientation exists on a spectrum of possibilities that may evolve throughout one's life journey.

Psychoanalytic thinking offers a valuable perspective on this fluidity, recognizing that there exists a creative, liminal space between inner psychic reality and external shared reality where identity exploration becomes possible. For those exploring sexual fluidity, this space represents the freedom to experiment with desires and identities beyond culturally prescribed categories.

When working with couples navigating sexual fluidity, therapy must balance competing needs: for security and stability alongside authentic sexual expression; acknowledging desire discrepancies while avoiding pathologizing either partner; and supporting identity exploration while recognizing its impact on the relationship system. The following case illustrates these complexities in action.

—

Case Introduction: The Story of Sophia and Shawn

"If I was a young person today, I would identify as non-binary and bisexual. It would be so freeing to have that kind of fluidity and not feel so trapped in the suburban norms that I grew up in. I would have the freedom to dress and move through the world in whatever way felt most authentic that day – sometimes softer, sometimes more assertive, sometimes neither.

DOI: 10.4324/9781003318187-10

And the freedom to explore my sexuality with females unapologetically would be a dream."

But before I had a chance to respond, Sophia continued her thought . . .

"God, that feels so ridiculous and indulgent to say out loud, let alone live my life like that."

Sophia had come in for an individual session at my request. We had hit a plateau in the couple sessions. I wasn't making any traction either moving the sessions forward or helping them deepen into themselves. This week I had asked to meet with them both individually.

"What keeps you from being more open with Shawn about both your true desires and your confusion?" I asked.

"He's going to want to talk about it and I don't have any answers for him and I know that will make him feel sad and upset. It's like when we tried an open relationship and he felt so sad after my dates. I couldn't bear to see him like that, so it was easier to just close our relationship and stop going on dates with women. In the end, I know that Shawn and I will be great parents together and I guess right now it seems easier to focus on starting a family. At least we can both be excited about that."

"Even at the expense of transparency, honesty, sexual satisfaction, and feeling authentic in your identity?"

Sophia started to well up with tears and let out a long sigh.

"I can't say for certain that I am nonbinary. I can't say for certain that I'm bisexual. Maybe I am heterosexual and I just don't like sex very much. Well okay, if I'm honest I don't think that is actually true – the part about not liking sex. But it's too depressing to think that I don't like sex with Shawn, when I know that I do love him. I don't see myself being in a committed relationship with a woman and I have never identified as gay, so I don't know where that leaves me. I love the excitement and closeness I feel when being sexual with a woman. But I also see myself as heterosexual; I just haven't ever really enjoyed sex with men that much. The one thing I am certain of is wanting to be a mother. And I guess that is as good a place as any to start. If I have to choose between becoming a mother or figuring out my sexual and gender identity, I guess my choice is being a mother."

This time I let out the sigh, but before I could speak, Sophia interjected:

"I know your next question, Juliane. What makes me think that I have to choose? And why couldn't I do both? Well that's the magic question that doesn't seem to have an answer – or at least not the kind of time I am willing to sacrifice to figure it out."

Sophia's monologue reveals a dynamic struggle between competing internal needs: the drive toward authenticity and erotic exploration versus the

desire for belonging, stability, and attachment. This tension is deeply familiar in psychoanalytic work, where unconscious conflict is often organized
around opposing wishes, especially when identity and desire are in flux.

From a Winnicottian lens, we might see Sophia's fantasized self – "a
bisexual 'them' with freedom of expression" – as a transitional expression of her true self. It emerges in the protected space of therapy, where
play and imagination can offer glimpses of identity that feel impossible to
claim in external life. Her rapid self-correction ("God, that feels so ridiculous and indulgent . . .") points to the presence of an internalized critical
object – likely a legacy of earlier relational environments in which deviance
from normativity felt dangerous or shameful.

Sophia's statement that she must choose between being a mother and
being true to her evolving sexual identity reflects what Jessica Benjamin
might describe as a collapse of thirdness – the mutual space where self and
other can coexist without foreclosure. In the absence of that space, Sophia
feels she must sacrifice parts of herself to preserve connection, replicating
an earlier attachment template in which compliance ensured safety.

Her longing for fluidity – expressed with both yearning and defensiveness – also invites us to consider Adrienne Harris's (2009) work on
multiplicity and the nonlinear nature of identity. Harris emphasizes the
non-unitary self as essential to psychological health, suggesting that the
fluid parts of Sophia's identity are not regressive but represent untapped
resources for self-expansion.

This particular session sets the tone for the work ahead – not only to
understand the erotic symptoms but to hold the space between knowing
and not knowing, between certainty and exploration, between what is and
what might still be unfolding.

Conflict Avoidance and the Illusion of Harmony

Sophia and Shawn came to couples therapy seeking help with a desire
discrepancy in their relationship. Recently engaged, they described each
other as best friends and spoke with warmth and excitement about starting a family together. And yet, it had been several months since they'd
had sex. Shawn expressed concern and a growing sense of disconnection. Sophia attributed her low desire to a mild depression and the stress
of work. "I know, Shawn, and I'm sorry," she said in our first session.
"I've been really struggling with my depression and work stress, but I'm
gearing myself up for a sex date with you soon." In their shared formulation, the problem belonged to Sophia – her lack of desire, her stress,
her delay.

They arrived in therapy well-informed, referencing Emily Nagoski's
dual-drive model of sexual desire. Sophia identified as having responsive

desire, and Shawn as having spontaneous desire. They had read *Come As You Are* in preparation for our work and entered the room eager to share their findings. They presented their insights with articulate clarity and what initially appeared to be emotional collaboration. But as I listened more closely, something about the formulation felt overly cohesive – like a story they had rehearsed together. It was as if they had found a satisfying conceptual framework before fully exploring the terrain of their emotional and sexual lives. Their use of psychoeducational language served to contain anxiety but also risked bypassing something more emotionally raw and unresolved.

In such moments, I've learned to attend not only to the content of what's being said but to the emotional tone in which it's delivered. As Ogden (1994a) suggests, the analytic third includes not just the patient and therapist but also the intersubjective field in which unconscious communications emerge. Something in the field between us felt overly curated and too neat. I sensed the presence of a defense – one constructed not out of denial, but out of mutual protection. It stirred a quiet alertness in me – a clinical hunch that something deeper was being smoothed over. Often, these subtle dissonances in the therapeutic frame point to material that is dissociated, disavowed, or not yet symbolized.

While Sophia and Shawn labeled themselves through the lens of responsive and spontaneous desire, the packaging of their sexual dilemma felt too buttoned-up, too free of friction. And this, too, became a clinical clue. They were both deeply invested in protecting the harmony of their relationship. Their dynamic was defined not by overt conflict, but by its absence. They anticipated each other's emotional needs with such care that neither seemed willing to speak freely.

From a systemic and developmental perspective, conflict avoidance can function as a form of collusive regulation – protecting the attachment bond at the expense of individual differentiation (Schnarch, 2009). What appears as relational maturity may in fact be a shared resistance to emotional disruption. In psychodynamic terms, their conflict avoidance reflected a mutual defense against loss – loss of attunement, loss of idealization, or the more primitive fear of abandonment. As family systems theorist Bowen (1978) would note, the emotional cutoff that occurs in families of origin often gets replicated in adult intimacy when the differentiation of self is underdeveloped.

Sophia and Shawn's avoidance of conflict appeared to preserve closeness, but it also blunted vitality. Withdrawal – emotional, sexual, or both – creates a wedge of distance. It maintains stability, but also stifles growth. And over time, this form of protection erodes authenticity. For Sophia and Shawn, the risk of hurting one another had begun to eclipse the possibility of truly knowing each other. Their intimacy was strong, but it was bounded by an unspoken contract: don't disrupt the connection by speaking what might wound.

As a therapist, I've learned to trust the quiet unease that arises in these moments. What's not being said often holds as much meaning as what is. The analytic task becomes not to rupture the frame with premature interpretation, but to remain curious – to slow the tempo, widen the field, and invite whatever hasn't yet been put into words to gradually take shape.

Tracing Desire and Dissociation

We spent several months exploring Sophia's and Shawn's sexual history and the nature of Sophia's low desire. It was difficult for her to talk about with any detail, and she often side-stepped the conversation by announcing that she would put a "sex date" on the calendar in hopes this would make Shawn happy. Shawn, however, was growing weary of their sex dates, which were often unsuccessful. They either didn't happen because Sophia wasn't "in the mood," or they attempted to be sexual without much actual enjoyment or pleasure in the experience. Shawn complained that it was obvious when Sophia was forcing herself to engage sexually with him, and it left him feeling frustrated and humiliated. This in turn reinforced Sophia's feeling like a failure and left her with a lingering sense of hopelessness.

From a clinical standpoint, this cycle of avoidance, disappointment, and shutdown mirrors what Sue Johnson (2008) describes in emotionally focused therapy (EFT) as the negative interaction cycle: a repetitive loop where unmet attachment needs generate protest behaviors or withdrawal, creating emotional distance rather than closeness. When this dynamic plays out in the sexual domain, desire becomes not only a physiological issue but a relationally embedded one – entangled in the longing for security, the fear of rejection, and the shame of not being "enough."

Sophia's repeated pattern of avoidance, paired with performative sexual engagement, suggested more than a desire discrepancy – it hinted at an underlying dissociation from her erotic self. Rather than inhabiting her desire, Sophia seemed to approach sexuality as a task to be managed, which is often the hallmark of internalized compliance. Her attempts to schedule sex reflected a cognitive solution to an emotional problem, revealing an effort to preserve the relationship at the expense of embodied authenticity.

We explored their childhood and family-of-origin histories, which added important context to the relational loop that was playing out between them. Sophia was an only child and grew up feeling an obligation to tend to her mother's emotional needs. She described her mother as intensely loving and generous, as long as Sophia complied with her mother's preferences and expectations. If Sophia deviated from their symbiotic union, her mother would become either disappointed and hurt or critical and shaming. Sophia learned early on in life that it was easier to comply with another's emotional needs than to assert herself and feel the associated guilt and shame that came with autonomy.

From a psychoanalytic lens, Sophia's dynamic with her mother constituted an early template of fused attachment, in which differentiation came at the cost of love. Her adult experience of sexuality with Shawn mirrored this tension – an ambivalence about asserting her own desire, fearing it would harm the relationship or disappoint her partner. Her bodily disengagement during sex reflected this deeper intrapsychic conflict: the push toward autonomy and erotic authenticity was quickly overridden by the pull to preserve emotional safety through compliance.

Shawn, on the other hand, was the middle child of five siblings and grew up in a Midwest rural area. He described himself as sensitive and tended to shy away from the larger family group dynamic, which he described as gregarious, playful, and loving, but also overstimulating for him. Shawn described feeling anxious as a child and preferred to spend time alone with his mother, who he described as gentle and warm. But her time was limited with a husband and five children, so he spent most of his time alone, wandering the vast fields behind their rural home.

As an adult, Shawn wanted nothing more than to find his soulmate and experience the close, loving connection that he longed for. And for him, this need expressed itself most through physical intimacy. Sex for Shawn was a way to deeply connect with Sophia and to lose himself in the emotional union and closeness that he craved. And Sophia was acutely aware of Shawn's needs and felt the crushing guilt and shame that she was failing him by her lack of desire.

Shawn's erotic script seemed to be shaped by a longing for attunement and emotional presence, likely rooted in the early solitude of his childhood. Sexuality became a channel through which he could seek the closeness that had once felt out of reach. But in doing so, he unknowingly positioned Sophia as the emotional regulator for his internal needs – a burden that echoed her own childhood experience of having to manage a parent's emotional state.

This mutual enactment – Sophia dissociating from her desire to protect Shawn, and Shawn relying on Sophia's desire to soothe his emotional longing – created a relational bind. Neither was fully in contact with their own erotic selves; both were operating from inherited patterns of attachment and survival. The more Sophia disappeared during sex, the more Shawn pursued; the more Shawn pursued, the more Sophia retreated. The erotic field between them became organized around guilt, duty, and disconnection.

In this context, what looked like a simple desire discrepancy revealed itself as a more layered, developmental dynamic. Low desire was not simply a symptom to be resolved but a communication – a refusal, perhaps unconscious, to engage in a sexual script that felt emotionally unsafe and personally dislocating.

The Open Relationship Experiment

I continued to have the feeling that we were staying too much on the surface or that there was something more that wasn't being fully discussed. And so I asked the question, "Is there something more about your relationship that we haven't yet talked about?" Shawn and Sophia gave each other a knowing look as Shawn said, "I guess we should tell her about the open relationship experiment."

The feeling of being stuck, confused, or blocked is a hunch that I have grown to trust in myself and asking an open-ended question like, "Is there something that we haven't yet talked about?" often yields new and significant information.

Shawn and Sophia went on to tell me that the year prior they had experimented with opening up their relationship. Sophia had disclosed to Shawn that she sometimes felt an attraction to women and often wondered what it would be like to explore being with a woman. Shawn was initially concerned and wondered if Sophia might be gay or bisexual and what that would mean about her commitment to him. Sophia assured him that she loved him and was committed to him, but there was something about breaking societal norms that she found exciting. She also found the idea of Shawn being with another woman exciting.

After several months of discussion, they agreed to experiment with dating other people on the condition that there be full disclosure and transparency on anything sexual that happened and that they needed permission from each other to pursue any potential dating partner. They both placed ads on a dating site. Sophia's profile immediately yielded a lot of attention, while Shawn's profile was slower to gain traction. They attributed this to Shawn pursuing heterosexual women, which required him to be more proactive in reaching out to women he found attractive. Sophia helped him write messages to women and in many ways acted as his dating coach, finding potential women for him and encouraging him to follow up with messages. Although Shawn had several exchanges with women, nothing materialized into an in-person date, which left him feeling rejected, unattractive, and undesirable.

Sophia, on the other hand, had several women reach out to her that she found attractive and interesting. With Shawn's permission, she scheduled several dates over a few months.

I could see the excitement in Sophia's eyes as she recounted the experience of having these dates. There was one woman in particular that she liked and had multiple dates with, named Mary. Mary was intrigued that Sophia was beginning to explore her attraction to women and excited by the idea of being her sexual guide. Sophia loved to come home after a date with Mary and tell Shawn all about it, relishing in the details of the evening and their interactions. And although Shawn was curious in some ways, he mostly felt jealous of Sophia's excitement and enthusiasm toward Mary. He worried that he was becoming more of a friend to Sophia, and Mary was becoming more her lover. I could see Shawn's face deflate as Sophia talked about the progression of their open relationship.

Core Erotic Themes and Unconscious Conflict

I found myself thinking of Jack Morin's concept of the Core Erotic Theme. For Sophia, the open relationship experiment had not just been about acting out curiosity – it had awakened something vital. Her dates with Mary offered a sense of novelty and self-ownership that contrasted with the safety and predictability of her bond with Shawn. But Morin's work also reminds us that these very tensions between freedom and fidelity, pleasure and guilt, autonomy and attachment are the engine of erotic energy. When we suppress that tension, we may find comfort, but we often lose our erotic vitality.

When I asked Shawn what the open relationship experiment was like for him, he replied:

I had some hesitation at first, but then the thought of doing something sexually edgy appealed to me. I envisioned it as something that Sophia and I would share together, maybe even have a threesome eventually. But honestly, I think that was just my sexual lust getting stirred up. Because in reality, it was hard to see Sophia get so excited about her dates, especially when not much was happening for me on my end. And Sophia seemed more distracted from me unless she was going over all the details of her dates with Mary. I know it was meant as a way to include me, but it felt more like a slap in the face and a reminder that I was on the outside of this new triangle that was forming. It felt like our relationship was fading into the background as Mary was starting to take center stage.

At this point, Sophia jumped in to say, "It became obvious to me that Shawn was having a hard time with the open relationship and that didn't make me feel good, so I stopped seeing Mary. We didn't really talk about it, but I could tell how relieved Shawn was when I told him that I closed my account on the dating site."

It was clear that Sophia's guilt was the motivation for her decision. It was the same guilt she had felt as a girl disappointing her mother, now projected onto Shawn. Jack Morin would call this a "conflict at the heart of desire." Sophia's authentic erotic self was reaching toward fluidity, queer exploration, and the freedom to play with identity. But it clashed with an equally powerful need to care for the emotional well-being of her partner. In Morin's language, her deepest turn-on was entangled with her deepest taboo – claiming desire meant risking the loss of attachment and triggering shame.

At this point, Shawn turned to Sophia and said, "Do you regret not continuing with the dates?"

Sophia took his hand and said, "Not at all Shawn. It was not a great idea to begin with. It's better that we just focus on each other and on becoming parents."

And while Sophia's words seemed genuine, there was also a sense of resignation in her voice.

Then Shawn turned to me and said:

It's just that we haven't really gotten our sex life back on track since then. Most of my college years, I fantasized about getting married to my soulmate and having a robust and erotic sex life. I used to daydream about what it would be like to have sex in the mornings before work and again in the evenings before bed and weekends would be checkered with lusty afternoon sex. I imagined being married as this great way of having all kinds of sex with someone who felt like your best friend. Sophia absolutely feels like my best friend, but our sex life doesn't match anything resembling what I imagined. I can't help but feel depressed about that.

It was clear to me that Shawn, too, was navigating his own emotional loop. His desire for closeness and emotional union through sex was real and heartfelt. But it also left him vulnerable to Sophia's shifting interest. When sex didn't happen with Sophia or felt disconnected, he experienced it not as a simple disappointment, but as a personal rejection. Like the boy wandering the fields alone, he felt left out and unchosen.

Morin's theory of the "Core Erotic Theme" suggests that the seeds of our adult erotic lives are often planted in childhood through the interplay of longing, frustration, shame, and secrecy. These early emotional experiences form a kind of erotic blueprint. For Shawn, being chosen, being held in a shared intimate space, and feeling that he mattered deeply – these were not just romantic desires but erotic ones. And for Sophia, the act of claiming her own erotic autonomy, outside of the roles she had been assigned, was equally core to her desire – but charged with anxiety and guilt.

A Moment of Honesty – and Retreat

At that moment, Sophia took his hand again and said, as she was crying:

> I'm so sorry, Shawn. You deserve that kind of sexual intimacy and connection with someone. You are such a loving and generous partner. It makes me so sad, but I will totally understand if you want to call off our engagement.

Shawn was also crying at this point and said:

> Being engaged to you is the best thing that has ever happened to me and I can't imagine wanting to be with anyone else. We are going to have a great life together and we will be great parents. We will figure the sex thing out, lots of couples struggle with this. I know that we will get to the bottom of this and once your work lightens up, I'm sure you will start to feel less stress. And we will go back to putting sex dates on the calendar. That should help with things too.

I ended the session acknowledging the deeper emotions that surfaced for them both. I validated their willingness to talk about the difficult emotions related to their open relationship experiment as a brave step in the direction of being vulnerable with each other. I used the opportunity to describe how vulnerability and conflict can feel uncomfortable but also provide a bridge to a much deeper understanding of ourselves and our partners. And through this awareness, we have the opportunity to deepen within ourselves and in our commitment to each other. My suggestion was to hold off on coming up too quickly with any "solutions" for this impasse in their sexual relationship and for us to spend more time becoming curious about and exploring their differences. I was hoping that this session would be a turning point.

But sometimes our best intentions are not met with equal enthusiasm. It seemed that the vulnerability and honesty was maybe too threatening for them.

When Therapy Ends Prematurely

Over the next few months, Sophia and Shawn had a renewed eagerness toward planning their wedding and used this as a reason to frequently cancel their sessions. When they did show up for their sessions, the focus was on updating me on the various decisions they were making related to wedding venues, guest lists, menu choices, and other details. They repeatedly thanked me for helping them through a difficult patch in their relationship. My subtle and not so subtle attempts at redirecting the focus of the sessions were met with a polite and unified resistance. The clear message from Shawn and Sophia was "No, thank you. We are done talking about sex."

And in fact, they were done. I received an email from them letting me know that they had decided to end therapy to free up time for wedding planning.

About a year later, I received a follow-up email from them with a wedding picture attached, thanking me again for all that I had helped them with and sharing with me their exciting news that Sophia was pregnant. I felt a lot of happiness for them as they embarked on this new chapter in their lives together and yet, couldn't help but also feel sadness for them as I wondered about the chapter that closed when they ended therapy.

Clinical Reflections: Holding Space for Fluidity and Ambivalence

The case of Sophia and Shawn illustrates the profound challenges encountered when working with sexual fluidity and desire discrepancies in committed relationships. At its core, we see the fundamental paradox of modern intimate partnerships: the tension between security and exploration, between the comfort of belonging and the vitality of authentic self-expression. When couples navigate the complex territory of evolving sexual identities, they often face difficult choices that therapy can illuminate but cannot resolve for them.

This case reminds us that developmental patterns from childhood powerfully shape adult sexuality, that relational safety sometimes comes at the cost of erotic authenticity, and that therapeutic progress is ultimately bounded by clients' readiness for change. The most valuable therapeutic stance in such work is one of compassionate curiosity – creating space for ambiguity, differentiating between identity and behavior, exploring the emotional underpinnings of desire, and challenging false dichotomies. By holding this space between knowing and not knowing, therapists honor both the necessary security of attachment and the vital importance of authenticity, even when clients choose paths that prioritize stability over continued exploration.

Summary of Key Concepts

- **Sexual Fluidity Is Relational, Not Just Individual:** As Sophia's story illustrates, sexual identity often emerges in response to relational dynamics, internal conflict, and the pull between personal authenticity and attachment. Fluidity is not necessarily indecision – it can represent an evolving truth that defies binary categorization.

- **Desire Discrepancy as Communication:** Rather than a symptom to be fixed, differences in sexual desire often express unconscious emotional dynamics, early attachment wounds, and internalized relational roles.
- **The Interplay of Erotic and Developmental Scripts:** Drawing on Jack Morin's Core Erotic Theme and psychoanalytic insights, this chapter highlights how adult sexual challenges are often shaped by early experiences of longing, shame, and unmet emotional needs.
- **Therapy as a Space for Thirdness:** Inspired by Jessica Benjamin and Adrienne Harris, the chapter underscores the value of the therapeutic space as one where multiple self-states, ambivalence, and emotional truths can coexist – without prematurely resolving tension.
- **When Clients Choose Stability Over Exploration:** Therapists must tolerate the limits of therapeutic influence. Clients may opt for secure connection at the cost of erotic growth – and this, too, must be honored as part of their agency.

For Clinical Reflection

1. In your work with couples facing desire discrepancies, how do you differentiate between a symptom of relational distress and a deeper developmental or identity-based conflict?
2. How do your own countertransference reactions shift when one partner expresses fluidity or ambiguity in their sexual identity?
3. When a client – like Sophia – expresses guilt or self-suppression in service of preserving the relationship, how do you help them explore these choices without imposing your own values about authenticity or individuation?
4. Are there moments in your clinical work where "not knowing" becomes a more generative stance than clarity or resolution? How do you hold this space with clients?
5. How do you work with clients who seem eager to end therapy after a vulnerable rupture or moment of insight? What internal reactions does this elicit in you as a therapist?

Chapter 10

The Unconscious as Orgasm

Sex and the Journey into the
Unknown

The Symbolic Language of Orgasm

What does it mean to surrender? In psychoanalysis, surrender is the act of letting go – of defenses, of certainty, of the compulsion to know. We surrender to the unconscious when we free associate: letting our minds wander across memory, fantasy, fear, and desire. In psychoanalysis, this unstructured process allows meaning to emerge rather than be imposed. The therapist's task is not to direct, but to hold – to create a frame capacious enough for the patient's psyche to roam, discover, and surprise itself.

This same kind of surrender is at the heart of sexual experience. Or at least, at the heart of sexual vitality. Orgasm, symbolically and somatically, can be seen as a form of psychic breakthrough – a release of tension, a culmination of energetic build-up, a brief suspension of ego control. It is the moment when the body, often bound by inhibition and expectation, lets go. In this sense, orgasm becomes a metaphor for the unconscious breaking through to conscious experience – an embodied moment of integration, of pleasure, of contact with something larger than the self.

To orgasm is not simply to climax. It is, at its core, to allow oneself to be moved – by sensation, by emotion, by connection. This is what makes orgasm such a fertile site for psychoanalytic exploration. When orgasm is blocked or absent, it may indicate more than a physiological issue; it may signal a deeper psychic impasse. As theorists like Thomas Ogden (1994b) and Dori Laub (1992) have suggested, the body often holds truths that language has not yet found. What cannot be said may still be felt. In this sense, orgasm – and its absence – becomes a kind of embodied speech.

For many clients in sex therapy, the struggle to orgasm reflects a difficulty not just with pleasure, but with presence. With letting go. With trusting another person enough to be seen in their most vulnerable and unguarded state. The inability to climax may reflect a disconnection from the body, a history of trauma, internalized shame, or an overidentification with performance. It is not uncommon for clients to feel their bodies

DOI: 10.4324/9781003318187-11

are "going through the motions" of sex while their minds remain distant, vigilant, or numb.

This is the landscape of sexual trauma – not necessarily event trauma, but the trauma of having learned, over time, that the body is not a safe place to inhabit. Shame, in this terrain, operates like a vice. It keeps the system tight. It forecloses movement, curiosity, and play. But when we bring shame into language – when we begin to speak what was once unspeakable – we begin to loosen its grip. As the body becomes a site of curiosity rather than judgment, new possibilities open. Orgasm may then emerge not as a goal to be achieved, but as a byproduct of connection – between partners, between parts of the self, and between psyche and soma.

The Relational Frame of Surrender

Contemporary psychoanalysis has deepened our understanding of surrender by situating it within the broader experience of relational vulnerability and trust. While classical psychoanalysis, especially in Freud's early formulations, centered on intrapsychic conflict and repression, contemporary theorists such as D. W. Winnicott and Jessica Benjamin have illuminated how healing and transformation emerge in the intersubjective field. From this perspective, surrender is not just a solitary psychic event but a relational achievement.

Winnicott (1971b) famously described play as the space where the true self comes alive – in the presence of a reliable other who can tolerate uncertainty and provide a facilitating environment. For sexual surrender to occur, a similar holding environment is necessary: one in which the body can relax, the mind can wander, and the self can emerge without fear of shame or intrusion. Benjamin (2018) adds that such mutuality is only possible when each partner is recognized as a subject in their own right – not collapsed into the other's projections, expectations, or needs. In this way, sexual surrender becomes a symbolic return to the developmental experience of being seen, held, and mirrored without demand.

Stephen Mitchell (1993), whose relational approach to psychoanalysis helped reshape our understanding of adult intimacy, saw sexuality not as a fixed drive but as a fluid, co-constructed narrative that evolves between partners. He argued that sexual dysfunction is often not about technique or pathology but about breakdowns in the capacity to inhabit shared erotic space – where vulnerability, attunement, and differentiation coexist.

In my own clinical practice, I've come to understand that sexual symptoms – whether they manifest as desire discrepancy, orgasmic difficulty, avoidance, or anxiety – often signal disruptions in this shared space. They are not just signals of individual impairment but expressions of relational impasse. When partners struggle to find safety within one another's presence, the body often follows suit – tightening, numbing, dissociating. Sexual surrender becomes impossible when psychic survival is at stake.

A psychoanalytic approach to sex therapy allows us to honor both the individual and relational layers of sexual difficulty. It integrates classical insights about the unconscious with contemporary relational theory and, when appropriate, draws on behavioral and somatic interventions as entry points into deeper work. Rather than reducing sexuality to mechanical function, it recognizes the ways in which early attachment, trauma, fantasy, and emotional regulation shape adult sexual expression. The goal is not simply to restore function but to create space for emotional truth, mutual recognition, and embodied presence to re-emerge – both within the individual and the couple.

The Case of Maya and Jack

Maya and Jack entered treatment because of Maya's low sex drive and difficulty with orgasm. Jack felt he was doing something wrong sexually and was eager to learn new techniques to help unlock Maya's desire. Jack was filled with enthusiasm about potential homework assignments they could do together. He arrived at the first session with a list of suggestions that he found doing online research and was eager to share with me and Maya.

> *Perhaps they could watch erotic videos together? What kind of porn did Maya think she might like? Maybe they could try tantric sex or role playing? Did Maya have any fantasies that she might like to play out? Jack found an app for couples that would match any compatible fantasies they both identified as being erotic. Maybe tonight when they got home from therapy, they could download the app together and get started?*

Jack sat in his chair, looking at Maya both nervously and excitedly, eager to hear her thoughts about his suggestions.

Maya, on the other hand, looked frozen. She had an overwhelmed look on her face and was trying to force a smile while she apprehensively nodded at Jack's suggestions. It seemed like Maya agreed with Jack in her mind:

> *Yes, maybe I just need to spice up our sex life. That might make me feel more in the mood. I remember seeing an article online with sex tips for relationships gone stale. I'll read the article for suggestions.*

But Maya's body was telling a different story. She had been experiencing a lack of sexual desire for the past year, which was understandably putting a strain on her relationship with Jack. They avoided the topic of sex altogether, and most nights Maya stayed up late with the excuse of needing to get some work done. It was easier not to go to sleep together in order to avoid the uncomfortable silence and tension that lingered between their bodies as they lay in bed.

The avoidance usually lasted a month or so, until Jack couldn't take it any longer and would erupt in anger, which included a list of complaints about Maya and how things had to change or he just couldn't see staying in the relationship any longer. This devastated Maya, who grew up in a home where threats were the standard form of expressing dissatisfaction and disappointment. It triggered in her a deep sense of fear, anxiety, and shame. What is wrong with me? I love Jack, why can't I just get turned on by him? I'm going to lose him if something doesn't change with me soon.

Couples tend to wait far too long after a problem surfaces in their relationship to enter therapy. This creates a build-up of frustration, avoidance, resentment, and loneliness, so it's no wonder couples often struggle with so much anxiety and hopelessness when entering sex therapy treatment. And at the same time, avoiding sex might also be a way to hold on and preserve the relationship. Sometimes attachment needs are more of a priority than sexual needs. Couples avoid talking about difficult topics to preserve the relationship and maintain the status quo. Ideally, sex therapy helps bridge the gap between attachment needs and sexual needs – and provides a frame for these needs to be normalized, identified, and managed.

So how does one help revive desire? Psychoanalytic sex therapy provides a continuum of interventions that span from talking to action. Recognizing where an individual or couple is along this continuum is a nuanced and inexact process. Therapy at its best remains flexible, when we allow for our curiosity to guide us and stay open to the unknown. When we are too confident in our answers, we run the risk of foreclosing important unconscious material, which can often be the culprit in maintaining a status quo position, otherwise known as feeling "stuck" or "shut down." Sexually speaking, this can look like low sex drive or difficulty having an orgasm. When this is the case, no amount of behavioral intervention will work. Homework, exercises, date nights, sex dates, toys, etc. all fall flat. In fact, it can add to a feeling of hopelessness when the desired results aren't achieved. Now we aren't only bad at having sex, we are also bad at sex therapy.

The Performance Trap and the Problem of Spectatoring

This is the predicament that Maya and Jack found themselves in. Jack became hyper focused on trying to "fix" the problem. In his attempt to help Maya, he got into the regular routine of forwarding articles with sex tips and suggestions for increasing desire. Jack's "help" was inadvertently increasing Maya's anxiety and her belief that there was something wrong with her that needed to be "fixed." Spectatoring is a phenomenon that happens when we get stuck in our heads worrying, ruminating, and overthinking. It distracts us from being in the moment and makes authentic connection impossible. When spectatoring occurs during sex, we find ourselves detached from our bodies and stuck in our minds, preoccupied and worrying about all kinds of things. *Am I too fat? Not toned enough? Smell okay? Is he turned on? Why isn't he kissing me? His penis isn't fully hard. I must be doing something wrong.* Spectatoring keeps us trapped at the performative level of sex and worrying about doing it right, rather than surrendering or being open to the experience of pleasure.

Desire, Anxiety, and the Need to Slow Down

I started my work with Maya and Jack by giving them a writing exercise. This exercise has been developed by psychologist and sex therapist Suzanne Iasenza. Each partner is asked to independently write down any and all of their associations to the words sexual, sensual, and erotic. They are asked not to share their lists with each other until the next scheduled session. During the session, we begin to have conversations about what they each experience as sexual, sensual, and erotic. This approach promotes curiosity about each other's sexuality, as opposed to trying to fix a problem. Having a problem to fix can reduce sexuality to a set of mechanical functions, which doesn't necessarily stimulate desire or arousal. Curiosity promotes interest in each other, which sets the stage for desire. As Esther Perel notes, "Intimacy" can be broken down to Into – Me – See. When we feel seen by our partners and approached with a sense of curiosity and interest, we feel validated. This forms the foundation of safety and trust, which for many people sets the stage for desire and arousal.

As Maya began to read her list, tears started to roll down her cheeks. Jack immediately offered Maya a tissue, telling her not to cry and reassuring her that there was nothing to worry about. I intercepted Jack's rush to "help" Maya and encouraged him rather to stay curious about what the tears meant to Maya. I was beginning to see how Jack struggled with holding emotion and was quick to take action on Maya's behalf, whether trying to "fix" her loss of desire or "help" her with uncomfortable feelings.

"Maya, can you tell us about the tears? Is there something that prompted the tears?" I asked.

Maya let out a deep sigh and said, "I feel so tired and lost. I don't even know anymore what turns me on or what I like sexually. It was so hard to write this list. And I just feel like such a failure." She then turned to Jack, with more tears streaming down her face and said, "I'm so sorry Jack. I know how disappointed you are and how frustrating it must be for you. This is supposed to be our honeymoon phase and instead I feel so dead inside." Before Jack could say anything, I intercepted by taking the lead and asking Jack to hold off from responding.

"Maya, it sounds like the whole topic and experience of sex has become incredibly overwhelming for you. You are trying so hard to reconnect with the sexual side of yourself, but all that you end up feeling is dead inside – like there is no desire there and nothing you do is helping to spark your sexuality. Is that right?"

Maya nodded. "Yes, that's right. And I know how much Jack wants to help me and I just end up feeling awful when nothing works to get me turned on."

"Yes, I get it. But let's just pause here for a minute, would that be okay?" I turn to Jack and say, "Jack are you okay for now? Would it be okay with you if I just stayed with Maya for a few minutes to help her with the list and to see if we can uncover some potential areas of desire?"

At this moment, I was intentionally creating space between Jack and Maya. I wanted to interrupt the pattern of Maya being the one with the "problem" and Jack wanting to "rescue" or "fix" the problem.

Once anxiety enters the sexual dance of a couple, it can take over and sabotage any chance of igniting desire. With Maya and Jack, the anxiety gets passed back and forth and becomes the driving force in stalling their sexual cycle and keeping them in a status quo position of feeling stuck. Surrender, pleasure, and orgasm can't happen when this anxiety cycle is active. The anxiety immobilizes desire. This is where the therapist benefits from stepping in to take an active role. This helps slow down the anxiety cycle and allows an opportunity for the unconscious material to get worked through. At the same time, the therapist is providing sexual education on desire and arousal.

A potentially useful point of reference here is to discuss Emily Nagoski's concept of a dual control model of sexual desire and arousal. In the dual control model, there is an accelerator and a brake. The accelerator is all of the things that work toward stimulating desire and arousal. The accelerator is essentially all the things that turn us on, whether they are physical, emotional, psychological, etc. The brake is all the things that turn us off. And what research shows is that our brakes are far stronger than our accelerators. The things that interfere with arousal make more of a lasting impact on desire and arousal than the things that turn us on. There are a variety of sex therapy exercises that work specifically on understanding one's sexual and erotic blueprint, for example, the sexual menu exercise that I asked Jack and Maya to do.

Understanding the Brakes: Pressure, Perfectionism, and Shame

While exploring Maya's reaction to the writing exercise, we discovered that Maya grew up in a home where there were high expectations placed on her with regards to academics and sports. If Maya wasn't as eager or enthusiastic about meeting the expectations or achievements that her parents placed on her, she was met with disappointment and emotional withdrawal. Maya recounted how her father made repeated comments on how much time he sacrificed by bringing Maya to her sporting events. It was only when she performed well or won her games that he would express admiration and pride. Otherwise, he lectured her on what she could have done differently to have achieved better results. This dynamic played out repeatedly in her life, not only in sports but in academic achievement as well. Maya grew up with the emotional burden of her parent's expectations, and the message she internalized was that anything short of success was a disappointment.

Once we were able to talk through Maya's anxiety and the internalized pressure she felt, we were able to make the connection that Jack's eagerness to "help" Maya felt much like her parent's expectation and their emotional need for her to be successful. Jack's help created the opposite effect, in that it triggered more anxiety in Maya and landed her back in feeling shame about her lack of success and the disappointment she felt from Jack. Uncovering this unconscious material alleviated some of Maya's internal pressure and gave Jack permission to step back and not work so hard at trying to fix Maya. Helping them both manage their own anxiety created some emotional space between them to get curious about desire and arousal.

Sensuality as an On-Ramp to Arousal

For the next several weeks, we worked on exploring Maya's relationship with pleasure and learned that there was little pleasure in Maya's life overall. And so the exercise was redesigned to develop a list of associations to the word pleasure. We decided that the exercise would be done in the sessions with me taking the lead, so as not to recreate the experience of pressure for Maya to somehow get the exercise "right." Jack was included as a helper to manage the list and write down what he heard, as well as to simply observe and listen to Maya explore her relationship with pleasure. Jack found this particularly interesting and satisfying, as he was relieved of his burden to solve this problem and could learn from watching me get curious and explore pleasure with Maya in a way that eased her anxiety instead of escalating it.

Initially it was even hard for Maya to talk about what might give her pleasure. She kept trying to link it to something sexual in order to feel like she was making progress on the exercise. She kept getting caught up in performance and trying to get it right. I would gently point this out to her, saying that she seemed to be in "good student" mode and focusing on her performance. This became a playful joke between the three of us, noticing when "performance Maya" was present and encouraging her to shift back to pleasure. However, even the topic of pleasure triggered a pressured reaction in her. So I took it one step back and shifted the focus off of pleasure and onto things that made her feel calm. She was then able to ease into the exercise a little more and focus on relaxation. We discovered that she felt calm and relaxed at the ocean or sea. She loved being near the water and taking walks on the beach at night. There was something about the sound of the water and the darkness of the night that felt soothing to her. She described an ability to tune out the world and her overactive mind during these night time walks.

Jack immediately jumped in with the suggestion that they could schedule some weekend trips to the beach over the next few months. "Slow down, Jack," I commented. "I know it's hard to resist going into action mode, especially when you are excited about a potential solution. But for now, we are in the discovering and exploring phase, that's it."

Jack struggled with his own sense of internal pressure to take action and find solutions. His impulsiveness kept him distracted from his own emotional landscape and from Maya's as well. For many people, emotional attunement is the precursor to erotic connection. Helping couples become interested in their emotions and the emotions of their partner can spark curiosity – and curiosity is often the first step toward rekindling desire. For many other people, another necessary ingredient in desire are boundaries. If we are too emotionally enmeshed, I can't differentiate you from myself. If I can't feel the boundary between you and me, my erotic flame can't ignite.

Maya expressed relief that Jack was able to take a step back and just listen to her. It helped ease her anxiety to know that she didn't have to have all the answers. She also found it calming to fantasize about walking on the beach at night. I asked her to describe the sensations. She spoke about feeling the wind on her skin and hearing the crashing of the waves. She spoke about the feeling of cold sand on her feet and the smell of the ocean. She described how the darkness and quiet of the night felt somewhat mysterious. Maya wasn't aware that she was describing sensual experiences and was surprised when I mentioned this to her.

"You mean that I am turned on by nature?" she laughed. "Yes, Maya. It sounds to me like your sensuality comes alive when you are taking these nighttime walks. Something about the experience of the ocean at night awakens your senses. Many people have an erotic connection to nature and it sounds like you might be one of them. It also sounds like there is something about the darkness and quiet of the evening that heightens your sense of mystery. This is another potential element of eroticism, that you enjoy being taken out of your routined schedule. Mystery is intriguing to you."

Maya's face lit up when I acknowledged how wonderful it was to hear her describe her sensuality. Then I turned to Jack and said, "I hope you are writing this all down, Jack. All of these elements belong on Maya's sexual menu list under her sensuality column. I think what we are learning is that Maya has strong 'brakes' when it comes to feeling pressure to be sexual. It seems that sensuality might be an on-ramp to her desire. And I think the most helpful thing you can do right now Jack, is to give Maya some emotional stillness so that she can tune in to herself and begin to discover how her desire shows up. Your job for now is to try and manage your anxiety and resist the urge to find a solution or fix this problem."

We began to use these foundational elements of Maya's sensuality to craft some interventions that Maya could practice at home. The process of crafting interventions or exercises is best done with a collaborative approach. It not only models constructive problem-solving but also increases the chances of active participation and buy-in from the client. The therapist can guide and structure the exercises after soliciting feedback and input from the partners. Instead of planning for trips to the beach, which would require potentially complicated logistics, we decided to focus on bringing the experience of the beach into Maya's daily life. I suggested that Maya experiment with taking showers or baths as an experience of relaxation and have a designated time when this would happen. Creating an experience that is intentional helps set boundaries, which in turn allows us to shift out of "work" mode and enter into "relaxation" mode. For Maya, this meant scheduling at least two 30-minute showers per week. These showers were not functional, and the intent was not to wash herself but rather to use the experience for relaxation. To create a sensual experience, the lights would be turned off and candles lit. Jack suggested turning on ambient music of the ocean and lighting a scented candle. Jack also suggested that he prepare the setting for Maya, so that she could simply walk into the already prepped bathroom and easily slip into the experience. In essence, they were creating a relaxing, spa-like experience for Maya to enjoy.

It felt so indulgent for Maya to be pampered like this, yet instead of resisting or rejecting the indulgence, she gave herself permission to enjoy the experience. She was learning how to give herself permission to invite and accept pleasure. There was no pressure to perform and no expectation of an outcome. It was simply an experience of relaxation and pleasure. The goal was to do nothing. It was meditation for the body. And for his part,

Jack felt validated that he could be helpful to Maya. Through witnessing Maya's pleasure and receiving her appreciation, he felt more intimately connected to her.

I also asked Maya to be aware of any thoughts, feelings, memories, fantasies that might come up related to the relaxation exercise. To begin to pay closer attention to her internal world of thoughts, feelings, sensations in her body and to be intentional about sharing her observations in therapy. Some people find it useful to keep a journal as a way to track their internal experience of thoughts and physical sensations.

From Sensation to Fantasy

Maya found herself daydreaming at work about the shower experiences and enjoyed the anticipation of her scheduled sensual relaxation. She also found herself feeling more sexual, particularly thinking about Jack preparing the shower for her. There was something about him setting up the room for her that turned her on. It felt like an act of service and a pampering that she hadn't before experienced. It was in total opposition to the emotional tone that she grew up with, which was one of expectation and pressure. She found herself fantasizing that Jack would enter the bathroom while she was showering, almost as a mysterious intruder. He would be so enamored by her that he couldn't resist entering the shower to touch her. Without speaking, he would begin caressing her body and giving her gentle kisses all over. The gentle kisses would become more intense and hungry as his lust grew. This would eventually lead to passionate lovemaking in the shower together.

Maya was initially embarrassed to bring up this fantasy in couples therapy, as she found it too exposing of herself. Yet she was also eager to report her success at feeling desire again. Her interest in being successful won out, and she made a few indirect comments about having some sexual thoughts as a result of the relaxation exercises. With some exploring and encouragement by me, she revealed her fantasy with both embarrassment in her growing sexual interest and pride at her progress in therapy. Jack found her fantasy to be very arousing and confessed to having similar fantasies of somehow participating in the shower experiences with Maya. After some conversation about each of their fantasies, they decided to act out the fantasy and have Jack enter the bathroom after 15 minutes into Maya's shower. They both agreed that there wouldn't be any pressure to have intercourse, as Maya felt like that might distract her from enjoying the sensuality of the experience. Jack was happy to accommodate this request. They also both agreed that if intercourse happened naturally, that would be fine, and they wouldn't intentionally avoid it. Their main objective was to play out the fantasy and see where it might lead them sexually. There was a playfulness between them as they both planned when the fantasy would take place and how it might unfold. They left the session with anticipation and excitement about the fantasy.

From Fantasy to Embodied Intimacy

When they returned the following week, they were both glowing and happy to report the exercise was a resounding success. Acting out the fantasy was highly erotic for both of them, and it led to lots of passionate kissing and fondling in the shower. Jack was erect the entire time, yet resisted intercourse because he was enjoying the experience of Maya's desire and wanted to keep the focus on her. Maya described being lost in the moment. All of her senses were being stimulated in a sensual way. The warmth of the shower, the ambience of the room illuminated with candles, the fantasy of Jack as a mysterious intruder all created an atmosphere where she was both calm and excited. She found her way back to desire.

Toward Relational Self-Awareness

Although Maya and Jack solved the initial problem of low desire, they continued in couples therapy to better understand and manage the relational dynamic that happened between them. They both had an interest in exploring their family histories in an attempt to discover patterns from childhood that were showing up in their relationship. There was a newfound curiosity in looking at their relationship through the lens of a multifaceted and complex web. They began to get curious about themselves in a way neither had done before, reflecting on their emotional responses to each other and making connections to their families of origins. They were developing what psychologist and relationship expert Alexandra Soloman refers to as "relational self-awareness," which is the ability to understand oneself in the context of our relationships, based on earlier relational experiences in our families, societies, and cultures at large.

For Maya and Jack, this was a slowing down and looking inward approach that didn't come naturally. They both identified as outward-facing and problem-solving types of people. Learning how to slow down, become introspective and reflective was a welcome experience. They both began keeping journals and began a practice of weekly self-reflection, writing down and exploring themes that surfaced in their relationship. They used the couples therapy to share their thoughts with each other, and I helped them both explore and make connections with their families of origin and earlier life experiences. They were both making discoveries about themselves through the lens of their relationship and valued the opportunity to reflect on and share these discoveries with each other. The value of this deeper exploration was a deeper self-awareness and therefore deeper intimacy between them. This would have been lost had I stopped at the behavioral resolution of the problem. This is the value of bringing a psychoanalytic lens to sexual symptoms.

Key Clinical Takeaways

Jack and Maya's journey reveals how seemingly straightforward sexual difficulties frequently stem from complex sources: early attachment experiences, familial messages about relationships, sexuality, success, and achievement, unprocessed trauma, and unconscious conflicts about intimacy. The psychoanalytic approach offers a framework for understanding these complex determinants without reducing sexuality to either pure biology or simplistic behavioral patterns.

When behavioral interventions are grounded in psychodynamic understanding rather than deployed as mere technical solutions, they can facilitate lasting transformation in both sexual and emotional realms. For Maya and Jack, the exercises became meaningful rituals of reconnection precisely because they were undertaken with awareness of the underlying psychological dynamics at play. Similarly, their communication practices became effective because they addressed deeper patterns of emotional engagement rather than simply introducing new techniques.

The integration of psychoanalytic theory with sex therapy techniques provides a framework for addressing sexual difficulties while fostering deeper intimacy and self-awareness in couples. This integrated approach honors the profound interconnection between psyche and soma, between emotional and physical intimacy. It recognizes that sustainable sexual healing requires attention to both the conscious and unconscious dimensions of relational life.

Maya and Jack's therapeutic journey illustrates how sexual symptoms, when approached with curiosity and depth, can become portals to profound personal and relational transformation. Their progress demonstrates that when couples are willing to explore the psychological underpinnings of their sexual difficulties, they often discover not only renewed sexual connection but also deeper self-understanding and emotional intimacy. The psychoanalytic sex therapy model thus offers a path not just to improved sexual connection but to a more integrated and authentic experience of intimate relationship.

Through this framework, sexuality becomes not merely a physical function but a rich domain of personal meaning and interpersonal connection – a landscape where our deepest vulnerabilities, desires, and capacities for connection find expression. The therapeutic work allows couples to reclaim their sexual relationship as a space of play, creativity, vulnerability, and profound intimate connection, qualities that extend beyond the bedroom to enrich their entire relational life.

Summary of Key Concepts

- **Orgasm as a Symbolic and Somatic Event:** Orgasm is reframed as more than a physiological release – it is a moment of surrender, integration, and embodied contact with unconscious material. Difficulty with orgasm often reflects psychic impasse, shame, or dissociation rather than dysfunction.
- **Surrender and the Relational Field:** Drawing from relational psychoanalysis, surrender is understood not as passive submission but as an active, co-created state that requires safety, mutual recognition, and emotional presence. This therapeutic and erotic surrender parallels Winnicott's concept of play and Benjamin's theory of intersubjectivity.
- **Spectatoring and Performance Pressure:** Disruptions in desire and arousal are often linked to overidentification with performance and external expectations. Spectatoring, or mental distancing during sex, reinforces shame and disconnection, especially in the presence of anxiety.
- **Sensate Focus and the Erotic Landscape:** Curiosity, sensuality, and attunement to bodily states offer alternate pathways to arousal. The use of mindfulness-based and experiential exercises – like pleasure mapping and fantasy exploration – supports clients in reclaiming erotic agency.
- **Psychoanalytic Integration:** The case of Maya and Jack illustrates how combining psychodynamic exploration with behavioral and somatic interventions creates a layered, flexible frame for therapeutic change. Sexual symptoms, when held with curiosity and depth, reveal developmental wounds, relational dynamics, and the unconscious conflicts beneath the surface.

For Clinical Reflection

- How do you attune to both the physiological and symbolic dimensions of orgasm in your work with clients?
- In what ways do you help clients identify and dismantle internalized scripts around performance, pressure, or achievement in the sexual realm?
- When working with couples, how do you determine when to intervene actively versus when to hold space for ambivalence, silence, or unfolding process?

- How might you assess whether your client's difficulty with orgasm is more rooted in relational dynamics, trauma history, attachment disruption, or body-based dissociation?
- Reflect on a time when a client's fantasy revealed something emotionally important or unresolved. How did you navigate your response – both as a clinician and as a person?

Chapter 11

Desire Discrepancy

When Arousal and Attachment Collide

Desire Discrepancy: More Than Just a Mismatch in Libido

Sexual desire discrepancies represent one of the most common challenges faced by couples in long-term relationships. At its core, what appears as a simple mismatch in libido often reflects a complex interplay between attachment styles, emotional regulation capacities, and relational dynamics. When partners experience significant differences in sexual desire, the resulting tension activates attachment systems that were formed in early childhood, creating cyclical patterns that can feel extremely difficult to break.

Research in attachment theory suggests that our early experiences of care shape how we seek connection and manage distress in adult relationships. Those with anxious attachment tendencies often seek reassurance through proximity and connection, while those with avoidant patterns tend to withdraw when emotional intensity rises. These attachment strategies frequently manifest in sexual dynamics, where desire itself becomes entangled with deeper needs for security, validation, and emotional safety. As Sue Johnson, founder of Emotionally Focused Therapy, has shown, emotional disconnection in romantic relationships often registers not only as psychological distress but also as a bodily and erotic shutdown – a somatic mirror of relational rupture. As we'll see in the case of Anna and Darren, these attachment strategies play out vividly: Anna's anxious protest takes the form of emotional urgency and sexual withdrawal, while Darren's avoidant defenses manifest in retreat, irritability, and a longing for connection that often bypasses vulnerability.

Desire, then, is rarely just about sex. It is a relational barometer, a bodily expression of one's capacity to feel safe enough to want, to ask, and to feel. Differences in desire often expose each partner's unique way of negotiating closeness and autonomy, safety and surrender. And when those differences

DOI: 10.4324/9781003318187-12

go unspoken or are met with shame, blame, or withdrawal, the cycle of disconnection deepens.

From a psychoanalytic perspective, desire discrepancies can be understood through the lens of unconscious conflict. In some cases, low desire may reflect internalized prohibitions around pleasure, a defense against engulfment or loss of self, or a reenactment of earlier attachment wounds. High desire, too, may be driven less by sexual urgency and more by unmet needs for validation, intimacy, or reassurance – needs that are more relational than erotic. Rather than labeling one partner as "low desire" and the other as "high," it is more useful to explore what desire (or its absence) is trying to communicate.

The therapeutic approach to desire discrepancy must therefore address not just the sexual symptoms but also the underlying relational patterns that maintain disconnection. This requires creating a space where both partners can explore their vulnerabilities without shame or blame. As Suzanne Iasenza (2020a) emphasizes in her relational approach to sex therapy, the goal is not to "fix" a desire imbalance but to understand its function within the couple's emotional system. This work demands patience, compassion, and therapeutic containment – helping partners locate the meanings, fears, and histories that animate their sexual struggles.

A Tense Beginning: Anna and Darren's Therapeutic Entry Point

"Just so you know, I am already three quarters of the way out the door and we have already tried couples therapy with several other therapists. Nothing seems to get through to Darren and this is my last-ditch attempt. I've been staying with my mother for the past two months and only agreed to move back in with Darren under the condition that he find us a new couples therapist and commit to weekly sessions. The first session he cancels and I am out."

Anna then turned to Darren and said, "I mean it this time, Darren. I have no problem living with my mom until we finalize our divorce. This is your last chance. And if you start this session by saying that I am frigid, I will walk out the door immediately."

I looked at Darren, who let out a big sigh and closed his eyes. I could tell he was trying to gather his thoughts, when Anna snapped, "Do you have nothing to say?"

This was my time to jump in and take control of the session.

"Okay, hold on Anna. Let me jump in here and ask you both some questions. I hear your anger, Anna, and I want to hear more from you, but first I'd like to ask Darren a few questions if that's okay."

This time Anna let out a sigh and seemed to calm down a bit. "Yes, of course. I'm sorry for just diving in and unloading all of that on you. I'm just at the end of my rope and don't know what to do anymore."

"Yes, I can tell, and I'm sorry. You are obviously angry, but I also hear that you're tired too. Let me see if I can help you." I took note of the tears welling up in Anna's eyes but chose to take the attention off her and focus on Darren for a bit.

In that moment, I made a deliberate decision not to focus on Anna's tears. Her vulnerability was surfacing, but it was tangled with rage, threat, and a clear warning that she might leave the session abruptly. I sensed that staying with her affect too long could flood the room or push the dynamic past the point of containment. I needed to stabilize the interaction before inviting deeper exploration. By turning to Darren, I wasn't ignoring Anna – I was trying to regulate the escalating intensity and protect the session from emotional collapse. Giving Darren space to speak also gave Anna a chance to pause, recalibrate, and remain engaged.

"Darren, can you tell me a little about what's been going on with you two?"

"Honestly, I am afraid to say anything right now. When Anna gets like this, I don't know what to do. Anything I say seems to set her off and I can't take the fighting."

"Can't you just answer her question without always twisting it back on me?" Anna snapped.

I jumped in again, "Okay Anna, let Darren finish please. You will have your chance to respond, but right now I need to be able to talk with you both uninterrupted, okay?"

I chose to step in assertively at that point to establish a therapeutic frame that could contain the volatility between them. Darren had just begun to speak – tentatively – and Anna's interruption risked reinforcing the very dynamic he was describing. By setting a clear boundary, I aimed to protect Darren's voice in the room without aligning against Anna. It was also a signal to both partners that this space would be different from their previous patterns: structured, safe, and intentionally paced. My goal was to interrupt the cycle of escalation before it took hold and to model a form of relational containment neither seemed to have experienced in recent years.

I turned to Darren again, "Darren, can you tell me what's been going on that has Anna so upset?"

Darren let out another sigh and responded, "We have been fighting pretty much nonstop for the past few years. It can get pretty ugly between us and I have a bad temper also. We tried going to couples therapy, but usually we just end up leaving the sessions not really feeling any better and going home to rehash whatever we were fighting about."

"No Darren, we don't fight about 'whatever.' The reason we are fighting is because you seem to think that we don't have enough sex and that it's my fault. I'm done trying to tiptoe around you and force myself to have sex that is painful, only to have you complain that it's not fun for you to have to go slow and be so gentle."

"No Anna, that's not accurate. What I complain about is that it's not exactly fun when you are blaming me for being too rough or not gentle enough when I am trying to do everything right and exactly how you are instructing me to. What's the point of sex if it has to be micromanaged every step of the way and I still get critiqued for everything I am doing wrong? And then I get threatened all the time with you leaving and wanting a divorce because you somehow think I am being too demanding or dominant or rough with you."

"Okay, stop, both of you. Listen, I can see how hard this is for you both to talk about. And it seems pretty obvious to me there is a lot of resentment built up between you. If you want couples therapy to work, we have to stop with the blaming and accusations and interrupting each other. If you can't talk directly to each other without interrupting, then please just stop and only talk to me. Seriously, I need you both to agree to some basic ground rules otherwise this round of couples therapy will just fail like your other attempts."

This second intervention was about establishing emotional boundaries, not just conversational ones. The mutual interruptions and accusations were pulling them back into their entrenched dynamic – one marked by blame, defensiveness, and emotional reactivity. I wasn't simply trying to referee; I was trying to create a therapeutic holding environment where each person could begin to speak from a place other than reactivity. By setting clear ground rules, I was also communicating that this work would require a different kind of effort – not just expressing emotion, but tolerating discomfort, listening without immediately defending, and making room for the other. In couples like Anna and Darren, where resentment runs high and trust is low, these small but firm interventions help build a structure that can eventually support more vulnerable and productive dialogue.

And so this was my introduction to Anna and Darren – two people caught in a cycle of longing and blame, both exhausted by the distance between them, and both quietly hoping that something could shift.

From a clinical standpoint, their opening exchange revealed several key dynamics common to entrenched desire discrepancy: threat, shame, protest, and emotional volatility. Their reactivity – Anna's rage and Darren's resignation – reflected not only their current sexual struggles but also deeper attachment injuries and years of emotional disrepair. As Terry Real has noted, couples often show up in therapy at the final breaking point, having defaulted to maladaptive relational stances: Anna's "angry pursuer" and Darren's "withdrawn controller" were classic enactments of protest and retreat.

The therapist's early task in such cases is containment. Without a firm and emotionally attuned frame, therapy risks becoming a reenactment of the couple's conflict. By stepping in early, validating their distress, and asserting structure, I was not only de-escalating the immediate tension but also beginning to model the emotional regulation and boundary-setting they would need to cultivate for intimacy to rebuild. These moments lay the groundwork for a reparative relational field – one where listening becomes possible and difference can be tolerated. Only after this groundwork of containment and emotional safety could we begin to address the deeper layers of their sexual disconnection – through embodied practices and gradual re-engagement with desire.

The Therapist's Role: Containment, Curiosity, and Countertransference

For the next year I refereed their weekly sessions, helping them learn how to listen to each other without becoming defensive and reactive and teaching them how to communicate their anger and frustration in a way that wasn't hostile and attacking. The work was significant. At times, I too felt the stuckness they brought – moments where my own feelings of helplessness surfaced, wondering if I was doing enough, or if I too might become just another failed therapist in their eyes. Learning to name and metabolize that feeling allowed me to stay grounded and helped me model for them what it means to stay emotionally present in the face of discomfort.

In cases like Anna and Darren's, the therapist's emotional experience becomes a central part of the therapeutic process. Psychoanalytic approaches emphasize the value of countertransference – not only as a source of potential distortion but also as a tool for understanding the client's internal world. My own frustration, fatigue, and occasional hopelessness mirrored what was being enacted in the room: a long-standing loop of rupture and failed repair. Rather than pushing these feelings away, I treated them as information. If I was feeling drained, might Anna be similarly depleted by years of trying to fix things alone? If I felt criticized or ineffective, could that illuminate something about Darren's shame and sense of failure?

Jessica Benjamin's work on mutual recognition offers a useful lens here. When partners in a couple lose the ability to see each other as separate but equal subjects – when each becomes locked in their own perspective, treating the other as a frustrating object rather than a fellow mind – conflict escalates and intimacy deteriorates. In this sense, my role was not just to facilitate communication but to help restore subjectivity in the room. This required more than neutrality; it required a responsive, attuned presence that could hold both their pain without collapsing into it.

Therapeutic containment, especially in high-conflict couples, is an active and demanding stance. It is the art of staying emotionally available while setting limits on destructive behavior. It means tracking multiple layers of communication – what's being said, what's being felt, and what's being enacted. It involves pacing the session, slowing things down, redirecting escalation, and building the couple's capacity to reflect before reacting.

Psychoanalytic couples therapy asks us to hold the tension between empathic attunement and thoughtful disruption. I could not collude with Anna's anger, nor placate Darren's withdrawal. Instead, I had to invite both partners into a new experience – one in which their defenses were named, their deeper emotions contacted, and their relational patterns slowly brought into awareness.

Pain, Performance, and Protective Strategies

I learned all about Anna's struggle with pain during sex and the shame and anger she felt toward her body for not cooperating with the desire that she wanted it to feel. I also learned about Darren's frustration and confusion about the rejection and anger he felt from Anna, as though his desire for sex was somehow the cause of her pain and the root of the problem. When I redirected them from lashing out at each other, they were able to slowly uncover deeper feelings of shame, guilt, disappointment, fear, and anxiety.

Anna and Darren had each adopted protective strategies which now created an anxious-avoidant standoff. In many couples, anger and anxiety are mirroring emotions – different expressions of the same underlying distress. Anger often emerges as a shield against vulnerability, while anxiety reveals the rawness of longing and fear. In Anna and Darren's case, Anna's anxiety about not being wanted, not being "normal," not being enough, often manifested as critical urgency. Darren's anger, in turn, masked his own anxiety – that he was failing, that his needs made him unlovable, that emotional exposure would leave him even more alone. Neither fully recognized that beneath their reactions were matching fears of rejection and shame.

From a psychodynamic perspective, sexual symptoms like vaginismus, loss of desire, or compulsive performance anxieties often represent embodied defenses. The body becomes a stage where unconscious conflict is played out. In Anna's case, her body became a site of both betrayal and protest – an unconscious refusal to comply with a sexual script that felt unsafe or alienating. Darren's repeated attempts to "get it right" mirrored the compulsive cycle of performance often seen in clients with perfectionistic or narcissistically injured parts. Both were stuck in a pattern of action and reaction, each hoping the other would finally "understand," without either partner slowing down enough to understand themselves.

What made the work possible was their willingness – however begrudging at times – to stay in the process. My role was to help them recognize the protective function of their defenses, while gently creating opportunities for disconfirmation. Could Darren risk being emotionally exposed without becoming angry or defensive? Could Anna articulate her fear of vulnerability without needing to shut Darren out? These were the deeper questions animating their sexual impasse.

In many ways, the couple was caught in what Stephen Mitchell might describe as a failure of mutual regulation. Rather than co-regulating, they were mutually dysregulating. The therapeutic task was to slow down their reactivity enough that they could begin to differentiate past from present, protection from possibility. As their internal narratives became more accessible and less threatening, space opened for new experiences to take root.

Nervous System Regulation and the Window of Tolerance

None of this happened easily or quickly, and it took a year of work to siphon off the anger and improve communication before either felt safe enough to consider reestablishing physical touch. As with all clients, I was mindful to check in regularly with them about how the sessions were going. I make it a point to ask if the pace feels right, if my feedback feels like the right level of intensity, if there might be a different direction that they would like to go in, if there is anything in the sessions that feels troubling, negative, or anything that is difficult to talk about. Engaging couples in a process that feels collaborative, inquisitive, and reflective helps them experience what a relationship that promotes safety, trust, care, and concern feels like. It is modeling the skills of a healthy relationship.

There was still tension between them, and they were both quick to anger, but they had also developed the capacity to sit with uncomfortable feelings without lashing out at each other and becoming reactive. You could sometimes cut the tension in the room with a knife as they waited patiently for the other to finish speaking. It felt like very hard work being in session with Darren and Anna and I oftentimes felt exhausted by them. It took a lot of energy having to constantly referee the sessions and maintain tight control of their interactions in order to keep the sessions contained and safe. But I was also impressed with their diligence in attending the sessions and the effort they were both putting into the sessions. I complimented them often on the progress they were making, acknowledging how hard it was for them to really listen to each other without reacting, blaming, or becoming defensive.

From a somatic and trauma-informed perspective, this early phase of treatment involved significant work on nervous system regulation. As developed by theorists like Stephen Porges (Polyvagal Theory) and Pat Ogden (Sensorimotor Psychotherapy), trauma and attachment wounds are often stored in the body and expressed through dysregulated arousal – fight, flight, freeze, or collapse responses. Darren's reactive anger and Anna's anxious withdrawal can be seen through this lens as autonomic responses to perceived relational threat.

What we were doing, session by session, was slowly expanding each partner's "window of tolerance" – a concept developed by Dan Siegel to describe the range of emotional and physiological states within which a person can function effectively. When within this window, individuals can access empathy, curiosity, and reflective functioning. When outside of it – either in hyperarousal (panic, rage) or hypoarousal (numbness, dissociation) – they lose the capacity for relational repair.

By modeling co-regulation – slowing my own pace, staying attuned to their affect, pausing when escalation occurred – I was inviting them back into this window again and again. Over time, they began to internalize this process, gradually tolerating more emotional intensity without reverting to old defensive patterns. Though the sessions could feel heavy, they were also becoming a container sturdy enough to hold their pain without it spilling over into attack or retreat.

Touch Without Pressure: Introducing Sensate Focus

As their nervous systems began to stabilize and their emotional reactivity softened, it became possible to reintroduce physical closeness through sensate focus – a classic sex therapy technique that has been widely adapted in contemporary practice to accommodate trauma histories, somatic sensitivity, and mindful pacing. These structured, non-demanding exercises are especially helpful for couples who need to rediscover touch without the pressure of performance or erotic urgency.

As their emotional regulation improved, they gradually expanded their capacity to stay within what somatic therapists refer to as the window of tolerance – able to feel discomfort without dissociating or exploding. After the first year of treatment focused solely on helping them build safety and comfort with each other through communication skills, we began to explore the idea of introducing physical touch back into their relationship. They both wanted specific homework assignments that they could do at home together.

I introduced the idea of sensate focus exercises – foundational interventions in sex therapy originally developed by Masters and Johnson (1970) that emphasize non-goal-oriented touch. The premise is to build trust and pleasure without the pressure of performance or arousal. These exercises shift the focus from performance to sensation, helping clients reconnect with their own bodies and with each other through present-moment awareness. Sensate focus is especially helpful in addressing issues of anxiety, performance pressure, and dissociation during sexual activity, and can be modified to meet each couple's specific needs and boundaries.

Clinicians introducing sensate focus may consider starting with fully clothed, non-erotic touch exercises and checking in weekly about boundaries, comfort, and pacing. It's important to frame these exercises not as foreplay, but as opportunities for attuned, pressure-free physical connection. Tailoring the approach to each partner's emotional and somatic readiness is key – some may need more structure, others more playfulness or permission to go slowly. Framing these as shared experiments can reduce anxiety and foster a sense of collaboration.

Darren was a "spreadsheet kind of guy" and tracked the fights they had, so he wanted to create another spreadsheet to see if the homework assignments would have a positive impact on their frequency of fights. After considering a few options, they decided to begin with homework that consisted of weekly short massages. Darren requested that the massages be given twice a week, and Anna insisted that they would remain fully clothed during the massages. This was a compromise they could both live with, and it felt like an accomplishment that they could agree on a step forward.

They did continue to complain about each other's massage styles, however. Anna's massages were too soft for Darren, and Darren's massages were too firm for Anna. But despite the complaints, they both agreed that the massages were a fun and relaxing activity to do together, and they both looked forward to this biweekly ritual together.

What was important clinically was that these exercises provided a structure within which they could safely experiment with physical closeness while maintaining control over pacing and boundaries. For Anna, who struggled with vaginismus and shame related to her body, the fully clothed massages helped protect her from feeling overwhelmed or sexualized too soon. For Darren, having a clear structure allowed him to channel his desire into a form of contact that did not risk rejection or criticism. Over time, these moments of contact became their own form of emotional repair.

We also created homework for each of them to intentionally compliment each other at least three times per week. This was Anna's suggestion, as she appreciated words of affirmation. It was difficult for Darren to remember this part of the homework, as he too didn't grow up with many words of affirmation, but unlike Anna, it wasn't an important part of how he felt loved and valued.

Anna grew up with a father who struggled with chronic mental illness. His personality was erratic, and she never knew when he would become manic and hostile toward the family. She lived in fear and anxiety of his moods and couldn't recall any memories of being complimented during her childhood. Darren, on the other hand, grew up as an only child of a single mother. His mother worked long hours, and Darren spent most afternoons and evenings alone at home. He discovered pornography at an early age and used masturbation as a way to cope with loneliness and boredom. He didn't need a lot of interaction from Anna and preferred to stay in his home studio, working on his photography projects.

Anna needed more emotional connection from Darren but went about it by demanding more time together and criticizing Darren's isolation from her. Darren felt like this was an invasion of his private space and would react by becoming angry and hostile. Darren's attempts at connecting with Anna were primarily sexual, which felt insulting to Anna, especially since she struggled with vaginismus and skin sensitivity around her vulva area. Anna wanted more than anything to keep the peace; however, she only had a certain threshold before her anxiety would turn to anger and the demands and criticism would resurface, only to keep this toxic interpersonal cycle in place.

At one point, we named what was happening between them using Terry Real's concept of *relational stances*: Anna in the "angry pursuer," Darren in the "withdrawn controller." Their cycle wasn't personal – it was patterned. Naming these roles helped reduce the sense of individual blame and increased their mutual empathy. It also allowed them to begin the slow process of reshaping their interactions.

And once they could see it that way, they could begin to soften.

Rewriting the Script: The Meaning of Arousal

It was a frustrating process for Anna to feel like she had little control over how her body would feel. It left her feeling frustrated and angry with her body, particularly her vulva and vagina but also other parts of her body, like her joints and skin. She would often break out in rashes or other skin irritations. Her joints often ached for no apparent reason. She frequently felt fatigued. She had a string of diagnoses and had long worked with dermatologists, nutritionists, physicians, and other providers to address her ailments. But most of all, she longed for a day where she would feel free and arousal would flow through her body – but it never happened, and she was beginning to give up hope.

These physical symptoms, when viewed through a psychoanalytic lens, suggested a somatic expression of deeper psychic conflict. Psychosomatic theory posits that the body can become a site of unconscious expression when the psyche cannot symbolically process emotion, particularly in cases of chronic invalidation, trauma, or shame. Anna's skin reactivity, joint pain, and fatigue were not simply medical issues – they were also potential symbols of a deeper struggle to feel safe in her own body and entitled to pleasure.

The days of tolerating painful sex for the benefit of Darren's sexual needs were over. She wasn't willing to grin and bear it any longer. But she felt like her body was enemy territory, and more than anything, she preferred to avoid the humiliation of a body that seemed incapable of arousal. Darren, for his part, was tired of having to hide and feel guilty about his natural excitement, desire, and arousal for sex.

One of the key therapeutic shifts in this stage of treatment involved helping Anna and Darren revise their internal "sexual scripts" – the unspoken beliefs they had inherited about what sex *should* look like. As Suzanne Iasenza (2020a) has written, transforming sexual narratives involves shifting away from prescriptive norms and instead making space for personal agency, difference, and authentic erotic expression. For Anna, this meant confronting and grieving the discrepancy between what she imagined her body "should" do and what it could actually tolerate. For Darren, it meant decoupling arousal from entitlement or rejection and learning how to hold his sexual feelings without pushing them onto Anna or suppressing them entirely.

I too felt the heaviness of working with Anna and Darren, hoping for progress to happen more quickly or wishing for more optimism in the process. It was important for me to give them both permission to be negative and for me to not shut down their angry, frustrated, and hopeless feelings, while still applauding their ability to show up every week for their massages and for couples therapy. In moments where my own countertransference crept in – feeling exhausted, discouraged, or overly invested in a "success story" – I reminded myself of the value of bearing witness. Staying emotionally present, even when progress felt slow, was itself a form of therapeutic containment.

It was important for me to hold the flicker of hope that they could find an erotic thread to hold onto.

Permission, Presence, and the Slow Return of Pleasure

I spent a lot of time validating the physical touch of their massages, helping Anna and Darren recognize that erotic intimacy does not begin with intercourse – it begins with presence. We often talked about expanding the definition of sexuality beyond genital contact and explored the idea of a "sexual menu" – a tool often used in integrative sex therapy to help clients identify a range of sensual, emotional, and erotic experiences that can create connection and arousal. It was important to de-center intercourse and emphasize that eroticism includes many different forms of touch, sensation, and play.

This helped shift the dynamic between them. Over time, Anna felt ready to explore more physical closeness. Eventually, she agreed to wear only her underwear during massages. She could feel Darren's excitement and noticed his erection through his clothing, but thanks to their earlier discussions and the structure of therapy, she was confident that this arousal would not lead to further sexual touch unless mutually agreed upon.

Clinically, this was a significant moment of boundary-setting and safety. By allowing Darren's arousal to be present without becoming a demand or directive, Anna could remain in contact with her own body without pressure. In the language of somatic therapy, her nervous system was beginning to associate touch with calm rather than threat. As Pat Ogden and Janina Fisher have described, trauma-informed work requires that the body be reintroduced to sensation gradually, allowing the client to remain in their "window of tolerance" – the range in which arousal can be experienced without triggering dissociation or panic.

For Darren, it was deeply healing to experience his erections without the shame that he was doing something wrong or harmful. Eventually, this trust led to a new kind of sexual interaction: Darren masturbated to orgasm while Anna lay beside him, gently caressing his chest or arms. It was a moment of quiet intimacy. There was no pressure on Anna to reciprocate, no performance expectation – just presence.

This moment was not about sexual achievement – it was about relational repair. For Darren, the ability to express arousal without fear of rejection was profoundly validating. For Anna, witnessing pleasure without being asked to give or perform created a new model of embodied intimacy: one rooted in choice, not obligation.

The slow pace of the sensate focus exercises allowed them to rediscover touch without the anxiety and shame that had been tethered to intercourse. The therapeutic frame offered them permission to be learners instead of performers, and the safety to experiment without fear. Each partner was finding their way back to sexual connection through mindful exploration and attuned witnessing.

Mindfulness, Masturbation, and Erotic Recovery

While Darren masturbated, Anna didn't feel pressured to perform, which allowed her to relax both physically and emotionally. In that spaciousness, she discovered that she often began to touch herself lightly without planning to. She was surprised to find her breasts felt highly sensitive to gentle contact. These moments were subtle but important – her body was slowly becoming a source of sensation, rather than shame.

These discoveries were fragile. There were still moments when Anna pulled away from touch or doubted whether her arousal was real or performative. Progress ebbed and flowed. But what changed was their ability to stay with the process – to tolerate these fluctuations without spiraling into panic or blame. That tolerance became a new kind of intimacy, grounded not in certainty but in mutual regulation and emotional resilience.

Clinically, these moments represent what D. W. Winnicott might call transitional experiences – internal shifts supported by the safety of the therapeutic frame and the partner's attunement. Anna's body, once a battleground of failure and frustration, was becoming a site of curiosity, choice, and soothing. Her arousal didn't need to be consistent or complete. It needed only to be hers.

We often referenced the work of Lori Brotto, whose research into mindfulness and sexuality was especially resonant. When the body has become a site of pain or betrayal, desire cannot be forced; it must be approached gently, with openness and patience. Brotto's emphasis on interoceptive awareness – the capacity to notice and interpret internal bodily signals – was central to Anna's process. She was developing the ability to feel into her experience without judging or rushing it. This capacity is core not only to erotic recovery but also to trauma healing more broadly.

These quiet moments, like caressing her breast or resting a hand on Darren's chest, allowed something new to emerge. Not fireworks or ecstasy, but presence, playfulness, and safety. In psychoanalytic terms, Anna was moving from psychic equivalence (where her body's failure felt like objective truth) to a more symbolic stance, where desire could be tentative, fluid, and real.

For Darren, being witnessed during masturbation – without pressure to initiate intercourse or protect Anna from discomfort – was quietly transformational. He too was learning to experience his arousal without shame or demand. Mutual masturbation, in this context, became not just sexual expression, but relational repair – a form of shared presence that honored the needs and pace of each partner.

Healing Through Mutual Attunement

Desire discrepancy is rarely about desire alone. More often, it signals how a couple navigates difference, tolerates discomfort, and manages unmet needs. For Anna and Darren, therapy was not a linear path toward reigniting passion. It was a slow, layered process of relational repair – of staying emotionally present, disentangling sexual scripts from shame, and learning to sit with vulnerability without collapsing or retaliating.

What helped Anna and Darren wasn't fixing the sex, at least not at first. It was learning to remain connected through hard moments without shutting down, blowing up, or walking away. So many couples enter therapy longing to get back to how things used to be. But true healing often begins when they accept that they must build something new: a connection rooted in emotional safety, honesty, and co-regulation.

Viewed through a psychoanalytic lens, this shift reflects a movement from repetition to repair. As Freud and later theorists like Stephen Mitchell have described, unresolved relational wounds often get unconsciously repeated in the hope of a different outcome. In this way, the sexual impasse becomes more than a communication breakdown – it becomes a living expression of erotic transference, in which each partner projects deeply held fantasies or fears onto the other. These enactments often take shape through projective identification, where one partner unconsciously pressures the other to embody a disavowed part of the self – such as neediness, rejection, or control – until both lose sight of their shared longing. Anna's early experiences of unpredictability and emotional volatility, and Darren's emotional isolation and retreat, were reactivated in their sexual dynamic

Desire discrepancy often functions as a projective field – a space where unconscious conflicts are enacted through the body rather than verbalized. Anna's guardedness mirrored Darren's fear of rejection; Darren's arousal was interpreted by Anna not as longing, but as pressure. These patterns weren't just about incompatibility – they were embodied enactments of deeper psychic structures. The task of therapy wasn't to "fix" their sex life but to decode what the body was expressing: grief, control, protest, and vulnerability. As those meanings became speakable, the sexual impasse began to loosen.

For clinicians, Anna and Darren's case underscores the need to integrate attachment theory, somatic awareness, and relational psychoanalysis. It also highlights the importance of pacing: moving slowly enough for meaning to emerge, while actively enough to keep the work alive. Sexual healing – especially when shaped by shame, trauma, or bodily betrayal – cannot be rushed. But it can be cultivated through small, steady acts of presence, permission, and attunement. In this context, the erotic becomes not just a destination but a practice of relational repair.

Summary of Key Concepts

- **Desire discrepancy** is rarely just a mismatch in libido; it often reflects deeper dynamics of attachment, emotional regulation, shame, and relational trauma.
- From a **psychoanalytic perspective**, sexual symptoms like low desire, pain during sex, or compulsive behaviors often function as embodied expressions of unconscious conflict and unmet relational needs.
- **Attachment styles** frequently shape how partners seek closeness or protect themselves from perceived emotional threat. Desire itself may signal unmet needs for safety, recognition, or autonomy.

- **Therapeutic containment** is essential in high-conflict couples, requiring active structuring, emotional attunement, and firm boundary-setting to create a space where vulnerable exploration becomes possible.
- **Countertransference** is a critical tool in understanding the emotional field between partners and therapist. Feelings of helplessness, frustration, or fatigue can reflect the couple's internal reality and inform therapeutic direction.
- **Sensate focus exercises,** when adapted for trauma and attachment needs, can help partners reintroduce physical closeness without performance pressure. These interventions must be carefully paced and collaboratively tailored.
- **Somatic and trauma-informed approaches,** including concepts like the **window of tolerance,** emphasize the importance of nervous system regulation in reestablishing safety and connection in sexual relationships.
- **Erotic transference and projective identification** may shape how sexual behaviors and desire are expressed within the couple, turning the erotic realm into a symbolic site of protest, longing, or defense.
- Healing occurs not through performance-based goals, but through **mutual regulation, emotional presence, and the revision of internal sexual scripts** – offering each partner a new experience of intimacy, attunement, and choice.

For Clinical Reflection

- How do you currently approach desire discrepancy in your work? Do you tend to lean more toward behavioral strategies, relational interventions, or deeper analytic inquiry?
- In what ways might your own attachment history or sexual beliefs shape your responses to couples who are caught in cycles of protest and withdrawal?
- How do you track **your own countertransference** – including feelings of frustration, exhaustion, or overidentification – when working with high-conflict couples?
- What are your cues for knowing when a couple is ready to reintroduce physical touch? How do you adapt **sensate focus** or other interventions to respect trauma and bodily autonomy?
- Are you attuned to the **nonverbal and somatic communications** that emerge in the therapy room when discussing sexuality? How might these inform your understanding of dissociation, shame, or desire?
- How do you help couples **decenter intercourse** as the definition of intimacy and instead co-create a broader, more attuned sexual script?

Conclusion

As with any journey, writing this book has been filled with challenges, obstacles, and unexpected surprises. More than anything, it has required me to trust my voice – even when uncertainty loomed – and to let go of the pursuit of perfection. "Done is better than perfect" became my mantra. In that sense, writing has been its own kind of embodied practice: showing up, staying with discomfort, and allowing meaning to unfold.

Through these pages, we've explored the layered, complex, and often contradictory terrain of sexuality – not only through theory and research, but also through the lived stories of clients and the felt experiences of the consulting room. We've looked not just at sexual behaviors but at the unconscious meanings, memories, and relational dynamics that shape and sustain them. Sexual concerns, as we've seen, are rarely just about frequency, performance, or technique. They are encrypted messages – symptoms of grief, longing, shame, attachment, trauma, and psychic survival.

Desire, from a psychoanalytic perspective, is never simply a drive or instinct. It is a construction – formed through early emotional templates, cultural narratives, and embodied histories. Whether we are exploring compulsive sexual behavior, erotic shutdown, identity conflict, kink, or non-monogamy, our task is not to pathologize or correct, but to listen. To listen beneath the symptom for the deeper story the erotic self is trying to tell.

When a client says "I don't feel desire anymore," the question is rarely just about sex. More often, it's about grief. Or power. Or fear of what might emerge if they let themselves feel fully. Psychoanalytic sex therapy does not aim to impose clarity but to tolerate contradiction. To hold the paradoxes of wanting and not wanting, of freedom and fear, of closeness and individuation. In the erotic realm, as in the therapeutic one, it is often the unspoken that carries the greatest charge.

Throughout the book, I've shared the theoretical frameworks that guide my work: Jack Morin's Core Erotic Theme, Adrienne Harris's nonlinear models of identity, Jessica Benjamin's theory of mutual recognition, Stephen

DOI: 10.4324/9781003318187-13

Mitchell's relational dialectics, David Schnarch's concept of differentiation, and the embodied insights of thinkers like Pat Ogden and Stephen Porges. These theories don't offer simple solutions – but they do offer tools for staying engaged when things get messy, murky, or unresolved.

Equally essential are the voices of contemporary sex therapists who continue to shape my thinking and inform my practice. Suzanne Iasenza has brought vital depth to the understanding of how clients construct sexual meaning – how desire, distress, and identity emerge through personal narratives, cultural scripts, and relational dynamics. Her work highlights the importance of exploring sexuality as a story to be heard and co-constructed, rather than a set of behaviors to be fixed. Ian Kerner's approach to analyzing sexual scripts is invaluable with couples stuck in repetitive cycles of frustration and misunderstanding. His emphasis on mapping the emotional terrain beneath sexual interactions – how partners speak, signal, withdraw, and long for connection – offers a practical yet deeply humane framework for working with desire discrepancy and emotional intimacy. Holly Richmond integrates somatic psychology and sex therapy in a way that centers embodied healing and sexual agency. Esther Perel challenges us to think about the erotic within long-term relationships, naming the tension between love and desire. Alexandra Solomon invites a relational self-awareness rooted in emotional literacy and cultural attunement. Emily Nagoski bridges science and empathy, helping normalize arousal variability and sexual functioning with clarity and care. And Terry Real brings a bold, direct approach to gender dynamics and relational honesty, integrating trauma work with intimate connection.

I am also deeply indebted to somatic trauma theorists like Bessel van der Kolk and Peter Levine, whose work has helped illuminate the body as a site of both memory and healing. And of course, there are many others – too many to name – whose ideas have expanded this work and will continue to shape the future of psychoanalytic and integrative sex therapy.

The future of sex therapy, I believe, lies in embracing this complexity. It requires us to move beyond rigid models of dysfunction or performance and toward a relational, embodied, and psychoanalytically informed practice. One that honors the body as a site of memory and meaning. One that welcomes conflict and ambivalence not as problems to be solved, but as invitations into the deeper layers of the self.

This work asks a lot of us as therapists. It demands emotional courage and a tolerance for not knowing. It asks us to examine our own discomforts, projections, and longings – not to eliminate them, but to study them. To treat countertransference not as a mistake, but as a message. It asks us to track our own bodies, to remain open to surprise, and to let ourselves be affected by the work – without collapsing into it.

And above all, it asks us to listen.

To listen to what is spoken.

To listen to what is unspoken.

To listen to what is felt, but not yet named.

In the act of listening – with care, with curiosity, and with humility – something new can emerge. A symptom becomes a signal. A moment of pain becomes a portal. And healing begins not with fixing, but with understanding.

There is no final mastery of this work. There is only the ongoing practice of presence, attunement, and relational risk. The willingness to be changed by what we hear. The commitment to create spaces where the full range of human experience – including the erotic – can be explored with dignity, complexity, and care.

Thank you for taking this journey with me. My hope is that these stories and reflections open space – for inquiry, for reverence, and for the kind of deep listening that allows desire to be not just spoken, but felt.

Addendum

Sometimes a Cigar Is Just a Cigar – The Case for Simple Solutions

Throughout this book, we've explored the intricate ways in which sexuality expresses the unconscious: how fantasies can reveal hidden conflicts, how bodily symptoms may encode trauma, and how desire itself can become a symbol of longing, loss, or transformation. At the heart of this psychoanalytic sex therapy framework is the premise that sex is never just about sex. And often, that is profoundly true.

But sometimes, it is.

There are moments in clinical practice when a sexual symptom is not a metaphor, not a reenactment, not a portal into early attachment trauma – but simply a physiological issue, a side effect of medication, or the result of chronic stress. There are also moments when a straightforward behavioral intervention – like sensate focus, scheduling sex, or psychoeducation about arousal – can lead to dramatic improvement. These "simpler" cases are no less valid, and the solutions they call for are no less transformative.

The Value of Pragmatic Interventions

A heterosexual couple in their early 60s presents with a sudden drop in sexual frequency. Upon initial assessment, the male partner discloses that he has been struggling with erectile reliability. Rather than explore unconscious fears of aging or castration anxiety, the first step might be to refer him to a urologist for a medical evaluation. In many cases, physical causes such as cardiovascular issues, low testosterone, or medication side effects (SSRIs, beta-blockers) may be at play. A PDE5 inhibitor like Viagra or Cialis, prescribed responsibly, can restore function – and in doing so, dramatically reduce shame, restore relational intimacy, and improve self-esteem.

Or consider a young woman experiencing difficulty reaching orgasm. She and her partner are emotionally close and communicative, but their sexual encounters are short and focused on intercourse. Psychoeducation about the clitoral network, along with recommendations for external

DOI: 10.4324/9781003318187-14

stimulation and extended foreplay, may unlock pleasure pathways that had previously been ignored – not because of trauma or repression, but simply because no one ever taught them.

These interventions may appear deceptively simple. But their impact can be profound. The relief of realizing "nothing is wrong with me" can undo years of quiet shame or self-doubt. It can also free emotional bandwidth to explore other dimensions of the self – including those that may indeed lead back into deeper, symbolic terrain.

Quick Doesn't Mean Superficial

In an era of over-medicalization, many therapists rightly worry about bypassing psychological meaning. But to assume that every sexual problem is deeply symbolic can itself be a form of overreach – or worse, a resistance to clarity. As Ian Kerner notes, "Sometimes the cure is not to go deeper, but to go simpler."

Quick interventions are not inherently superficial. On the contrary, they may create the conditions for greater emotional accessibility. When sexual pain is resolved through pelvic floor therapy, or when desire returns after switching antidepressants, the shift in erotic vitality often ripples outward – transforming not only the bedroom but also one's sense of agency and relational engagement.

In these cases, the role of the therapist may be less about interpretation and more about knowing when to refer, when to educate, and when to simply normalize the wide range of sexual variation and function.

Knowing When to Go Deeper – And When Not To

How do we know when a symptom is "just a symptom"? The answer lies in the client's own narrative. If a symptom is clearly situational, if it is new or linked to a medication change, or if the client expresses little shame or emotional charge around it, a simpler path may be warranted. On the other hand, if the symptom is chronic, layered with affect, or interwoven with relational patterns, a more analytic exploration is likely to yield deeper healing.

Clinicians must learn to toggle between lenses: to think psychologically, medically, relationally, behaviorally, and somatically. Sometimes these frameworks overlap, and sometimes one holds the key while others remain in the background. It's less about choosing one over the other and more about cultivating clinical discernment – knowing when to sit in the unknown, and when to offer a practical solution.

Integration, Not Opposition

This chapter is not an argument against psychoanalytic sex therapy – it's an extension of it. To truly meet clients where they are, we must be agile. This includes the capacity to recognize when the path to sexual health is through emotional insight, and when it is through hormonal labs, vibrators, or permission to schedule sex without guilt.

As Esther Perel reminds us, the erotic is not one thing. It is playful, embodied, symbolic, practical, and social. To honor its complexity, we must hold space for both the mysteries of the unconscious and the straightforward wisdom of the body.

Because sometimes, a cigar really is just a cigar. And sometimes, the most straightforward solution is the wisest choice to make.

Bibliography

Anzieu, D. (1989). *The skin ego* (C. Turner, Trans.). Yale University Press.

Aron, L. (1996). *A meeting of minds: Mutuality in psychoanalysis*. Analytic Press.

Bader, M. (2002). *Arousal: The secret logic of sexual fantasies*. Thomas Dunne Books.

Bancroft, J., & Janssen, E. (2000). The dual control model of male sexual response: A theoretical approach to centrally mediated erectile dysfunction. *Neuroscience and Biobehavioral Reviews*, 24(5), 571–579. https://doi.org/10.1016/S0149-7634(00)00031-0

Benjamin, J. (1988). *The bonds of love: Psychoanalysis, feminism, and the problem of domination*. Pantheon Books.

Benjamin, J. (1990). *The bonds of love: Psychoanalysis, feminism, and the problem of domination*. Pantheon Books.

Benjamin, J. (1995). *Like subjects, love objects: Essays on recognition and sexual difference*. Yale University Press.

Benjamin, J. (2004). Beyond doer and done to: An intersubjective view of thirdness. *Psychoanalytic Quarterly*, 73(1), 5–46. https://doi.org/10.1002/j.2167-4086.2004.tb00151.x

Benjamin, J. (2018). *Beyond doer and done to: Recognition theory, intersubjectivity, and the third*. Routledge.

Bollas, C. (1987). *The shadow of the object: Psychoanalysis of the unthought known*. Columbia University Press.

Bowen, M. (1978). *Family therapy in clinical practice*. Jason Aronson.

Bowlby, J. (1982). *Attachment and loss: Volume 1. Attachment* (2nd ed.). Basic Books (Original work published 1969).

Braun-Harvey, D., & Vigorito, M. A. (2016). *Treating out of control sexual behavior: Rethinking sex addiction*. Springer Publishing Company.

Bromberg, P. M. (1998). *Standing in the spaces: Essays on clinical process, trauma, and dissociation*. Analytic Press.

Bromberg, P. M. (2006). *Awakening the dreamer: Clinical journeys*. Analytic Press.

Brotto, L. A. (2018). *Better sex through mindfulness: How women can cultivate desire*. Greystone Books.

Bucci, W. (1997). *Psychoanalysis and cognitive science: A multiple code theory*. Guilford Press.

Butler, J. (1990). *Gender trouble: Feminism and the subversion of identity*. Routledge.

Caruth, C. (1996). *Unclaimed experience: Trauma, narrative, and history*. Johns Hopkins University Press.

Casement, P. (1991). *Learning from the patient.* Guilford Press.

Diamond, L. M. (2008). *Sexual fluidity: Understanding women's love and desire.* Harvard University Press.

Dodson, B. (1996). *Sex for one: The joy of selfloving.* Crown Publishing.

Fern, J. (2020). *Polysecure: Attachment, trauma and consensual nonmonogamy.* Thornapple Press.

Fisher, J. (2017). *Healing the fragmented selves of trauma survivors: Overcoming internal self-alienation.* Routledge.

Fisher, J. (2021). *Transforming the living legacy of trauma: A workbook for survivors and therapists.* PESI Publishing & Media.

Freud, S. (1914/1958). Remembering, repeating and working-through (Further recommendations on the technique of psycho-analysis II). In J. Strachey (Ed. & Trans.), *The standard edition of the complete psychological works of Sigmund Freud* (Vol. 12, pp. 145–156). Hogarth Press.

Freud, S. (1917). Mourning and melancholia. In J. Strachey (Ed. & Trans.), *The standard edition of the complete psychological works of Sigmund Freud* (Vol. 14, pp. 243–258). Hogarth Press (Original work published 1915–1917).

Freud, S. (1920). *Beyond the pleasure principle* (J. Strachey, Trans.). W. W. Norton & Company (Original work published 1920).

Freud, S. (2000). *Three essays on the theory of sexuality* (J. Strachey, Trans.). Basic Books (Original work published 1905).

Harris, A. (1996). Gender as soft assembly. In M. Dimen & V. Goldner (Eds.), *Gender in psychoanalytic space: Between clinic and culture* (pp. 15–34). Other Press.

Harris, A. (2005). Intersubjectivity and gender: Making space for difference. *Psychoanalytic Dialogues, 15*(6), 829–854. https://doi.org/10.1080/10481881509348828

Harris, A. (2009). Gender as soft assembly. *Studies in Gender and Sexuality, 10*(1), 7–28. https://doi.org/10.1080/15240650902749384

Hazan, C., & Shaver, P. (1987). Romantic love conceptualized as an attachment process. *Journal of Personality and Social Psychology, 52*(3), 511–524.

Iasenza, S. (2010). What is queer about sex? Expanding sexual frames in theory and practice. *Journal of Homosexuality, 57*(1), 3–24.

Iasenza, S. (2020a). *Transforming sexual narratives: A relational approach to sex therapy.* Routledge.

Iasenza, S. (2020b). *Transforming sex therapy: Clinical principles for sexual wellness.* Routledge.

Johnson, S. M. (2008). *Hold me tight: Seven conversations for a lifetime of love.* Little, Brown.

Kaplan, H. S. (1974). *The new sex therapy: Active treatment of sexual dysfunctions.* Brunner/Mazel.

Kauppi, M. (2021). *Polyamory: A clinical toolkit for therapists (and their clients).* Rowman & Littlefield.

Kernberg, O. F. (1975). *Borderline conditions and pathological narcissism.* Jason Aronson.

Kerner, I. (2004). *She comes first: The thinking man's guide to pleasuring a woman.* ReganBooks.

Kerner, I. (2021). *So tell me about the last time you had sex: Laying bare and learning to repair our love lives.* Grand Central Life & Style.

Klein, M. (2010). *America's war on sex: The attack on law, lust, and liberty* (Rev. ed.). Praeger.

Kleinplatz, P. J. (Ed.). (2012). *New directions in sex therapy: Innovations and alternatives* (2nd ed.). Routledge.

Kohut, H. (1971). *The analysis of the self: A systematic approach to the psychoanalytic treatment of narcissistic personality disorders.* International Universities Press.

Laplanche, J. (1999). *Essays on otherness* (J. Fletcher, Trans.). Routledge (Original work published 1992).

Laub, D. (1992). Bearing witness or the vicissitudes of listening. In S. Felman & D. Laub (Eds.) *Testimony: Crises of witnessing in literature, psychoanalysis, and history* (pp. 57–74). Routledge.

Lehmiller, J. J. (2018). *Tell me what you want: The science of sexual desire and how it can help you improve your sex life.* Da Capo Lifelong Books.

Levine, P. A. (1997). *Waking the tiger: Healing trauma.* North Atlantic Books.

Ley, D. J. (2012). *The myth of sex addiction.* Rowman & Littlefield.

Lorde, A. (1978). *Uses of the erotic: The erotic as power.* Kore Press.

Masters, W. H., & Johnson, V. E. (1970). *Human sexual inadequacy.* Little, Brown and Company.

McDougall, J. (1986). *Theatres of the body: A psychoanalytic approach to psychosomatic illness.* W. W. Norton & Company.

McWilliams, N. (2011). *Psychoanalytic diagnosis: Understanding personality structure in the clinical process* (2nd ed.). Guilford Press.

Meadow, P. (1995a). The sexual acting out of the countertransference. *Journal of the American Academy of Psychoanalysis, 23*(2), 243–255.

Meadow, P. (1995b). The erotic body and the drama of narcissism. *Psychoanalytic Dialogues, 5*(4), 499–521. https://doi.org/10.1080/10481889509539067

Meadow, P. (2003). *The embodied analyst: From the art of listening to the physiology of expression.* [Published lecture material].

Mikulincer, M., & Shaver, P. R. (2007). *Attachment in adulthood: Structure, dynamics, and change.* Guilford Press.

Mitchell, S. A. (1993). *Hope and dread in psychoanalysis.* Basic Books.

Mitchell, S. A. (2002). *Can love last? The fate of romance over time.* W. W. Norton & Company.

Morin, J. (1995). *The erotic mind: Unlocking the inner sources of sexual passion and fulfillment.* Harper Perennial.

Nagoski, E. (2015). *Come as you are: The surprising new science that will transform your sex life.* Simon & Schuster.

Nelson, T. (2013). *The new monogamy: Redefining your relationship after infidelity.* New Harbinger Publications.

Nichols, M. (2020). *The modern clinical guide to sexuality: Integrating sex positivity, trauma-informed care, and neurobiology.* Routledge.

Ogden, P. (2006). *Trauma and the body: A sensorimotor approach to psychotherapy.* W. W. Norton & Company.

Ogden, P., & Fisher, J. (2009). *Sensorimotor psychotherapy: Interventions for trauma and attachment.* W. W. Norton & Company.

Ogden, P., Minton, K., & Pain, C. (2006). *Trauma and the body: A sensorimotor approach to psychotherapy.* W. W. Norton & Company.

Ogden, T. H. (1994a). *Subjects of analysis.* Jason Aronson.

Ogden, T. H. (1994b). The analytic third: Working with intersubjective clinical facts. *International Journal of Psycho-Analysis, 75,* 3–19.

OMGYES. (n.d. a). *Research-based techniques for women's sexual pleasure.* https://www.omgyes.com

OMGYES. (n.d. b). *The science of women's pleasure.* https://www.omgyes.com/

Ortmann, D., & Sprott, R. A. (2013). *Sexual outsiders: Understanding BDSM sexualities and communities.* Rowman & Littlefield.

Perel, E. (2006). *Mating in captivity: Unlocking erotic intelligence.* HarperCollins.

Perel, E. (2007). *Mating in captivity: Unlocking erotic intelligence.* Harper Perennial.

Perel, E. (n.d.). *Talks and interviews.* https://www.estherperel.com

Porges, S. W. (2011). *The polyvagal theory: Neurophysiological foundations of emotions, attachment, communication, and self-regulation.* W. W. Norton & Company.

Porges, S. W. (2017). *The pocket guide to the polyvagal theory: The transformative power of feeling safe.* W. W. Norton & Company.

Prause, N., & Ley, D. (2017). The clinical and social science of problematic sexual behavior. In P. J. Kleinplatz (Ed.), *New directions in sex therapy: Innovations and alternatives* (2nd ed., pp. 227–243). Routledge.

Queen, C. (1997). *Real live nude girl: Chronicles of sex-positive culture.* Cleis Press.

Real, T. (2007). *The new rules of marriage: What you need to know to make love work.* Ballantine Books.

Richmond, H. (2021). *Reclaiming pleasure: A sex-positive guide for moving past sexual trauma and living a passionate life.* New Harbinger Publications.

Rothschild, B. (2000). *The body remembers: The psychophysiology of trauma and trauma treatment.* W. W. Norton & Company.

Rubin, G. (1984). Thinking sex: Notes for a radical theory of the politics of sexuality. In C. S. Vance (Ed.), *Pleasure and danger: Exploring female sexuality* (pp. 267–319). Routledge & Kegan Paul.

Schnarch, D. (2009). *Intimacy & desire: Awaken the passion in your relationship.* Beaufort Books.

Schore, A. N. (2003). *Affect dysregulation and disorders of the self.* W. W. Norton & Company.

Simon, W., & Gagnon, J. H. (2003). *Sexual conduct: The social sources of human sexuality* (2nd ed.). Aldine Transaction.

Snyder, S. H. (2018). *Love worth making: How to have ridiculously great sex in a long-lasting relationship.* St. Martin's Press.

Solomon, A. H. (2017). *Loving bravely: Twenty lessons of self-discovery to help you get the love you want.* New Harbinger Publications.

Solomon, A. H. (2020). *Taking sexy back: How to own your sexuality and create the relationships you want.* New Harbinger Publications.

Spotnitz, H. (1961). *Modern psychoanalysis of the schizophrenic patient: Theory of the technique.* Grune & Stratton.

van der Kolk, B. (2014). *The body keeps the score: Brain, mind, and body in the healing of trauma.* Viking.

Winnicott, D. W. (1960). Ego distortion in terms of true and false self. In *The maturational processes and the facilitating environment* (pp. 140–152). International Universities Press.

Winnicott, D. W. (1965). *The maturational processes and the facilitating environment: Studies in the theory of emotional development.* International Universities Press.

Winnicott, D. W. (1971a). Transitional objects and transitional phenomena. In *Playing and reality* (pp. 1–34). Routledge.

Winnicott, D. W. (1971b). *Playing and reality.* Routledge.

Index

spectatoring 132–133
structure 72–73
supervision 12–15, 22–25, 50–51
surrender 3–4, 35–37, 45, 68–69,
74–76, 129–131, 141
symbolic language of orgasm 129–130
symbolic meaning 81–82

technology 10, 11
termination 112–114
therapeutic crisis 96–98
therapeutic healing: childhood
patterns and present dynamics
44–45; clinical case 41–44; clinical
reflection 51; consent 40–41,
45–50; countertransference 46, 50,
51; embodiment 39, 50, 51; erotic
templates 41, 50; power 39–40,
45–50; reenactment 40–41, 47, 50;
relational healing 49–50; repair
49, 50; sexuality 39, 48–50, 51;
theoretical framework 39–41
therapeutic mourning 112–114
therapist: courage of 23–24; role of
147–148; therapist comfort 11–12;
when the therapists' body knows
first 20–21
touch 150–152
transference 12, 17, 27–29, 32, 35,
94–95, 156–157
transformation 101–102
trauma and sexuality: the body as site
of healing 52; clinical reflection
38, 63; clinical vignette 30–36,
53–58; dissociated self-states 60,
62; and the erotic body 28–30; grip
of narcissism 26–27; integration
and completion 61–62; integrating
narcissism and sexuality 36–37;
language of the body 60–61;
masturbation 52–54, 56–62;
memory 52–54, 58–61, 62–63;

pleasure 52–53, 58–59, 61, 63;
positive narcissism and early
development 27–28; reclaiming
pleasure 53; solitary sexual
practices 57–58, 61, 62; somatic
reprocessing 58–60, 62; trauma
release 98–100

unconscious: anxiety 133–134;
brakes 135; case study 131–132;
clinical takeaways 140–141; desire
133–134; from fantasy to embodied
intimacy 139; need to slow down
133–134; performance trap and
problem of spectatoring 132–133;
relational frame of surrender
130–131; relational self-awareness
139–140; from sensation to fantasy
138–139; sensuality as on-ramp to
arousal 135–138; symbolic language
of orgasm 129–130

van der Kolk, B. 2, 5, 32, 52, 58, 60,
81, 159

window of tolerance 149–150
Winnicott, D. W. 27, 55–58, 61, 95,
98, 108, 119, 130, 141, 155
wisdom of the body: the body as site
of healing 52; clinical reflection 63;
clinical vignette 53–58; dissociated
self-states 60, 62; integration and
completion 61–62; language of the
body 60–61; masturbation 52–54,
56–62; memory 52–54, 58–61,
62–63; pleasure 52–53, 58–59, 61,
63; reclaiming pleasure 53; solitary
sexual practices 57–58, 61, 62;
somatic reprocessing 58–60, 62;
trauma 52–62

young adults 8–9

For Product Safety Concerns and Information please contact our EU
representative GPSR@taylorandfrancis.com
Taylor & Francis Verlag GmbH, Kaufingerstraße 24, 80331 München, Germany

www.ingramcontent.com/pod-product-compliance
Lightning Source LLC
Chambersburg PA
CBHW052008270326
41929CB00015B/2837

9 7 8 1 0 3 2 3 2 7 3 0 3